Perfect
romance

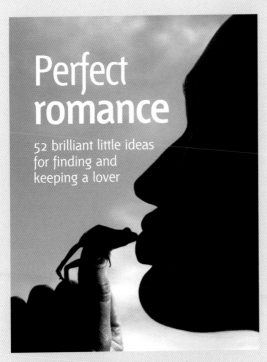

Perfect
romance

52 brilliant little ideas
for finding and
keeping a lover

Sabina Dosani, Lisa Helmanis
& Peter Cross

brilliantideas

CAREFUL NOW

Follow the tips in this book and you should find yourself well on the way to getting the relationship you want. However, there are no guarantees in life so if things don't go your way first time we can't be held responsible. Make sure you treat your beloved (or your intended beloved) with care and respect and if he or she isn't happy with any of the ideas you want to try out go slow and don't pressurise. We're sure you'll get there in the end – good luck!

Infinite ideas would like to thank Peter Cross, Sabina Dosani, Lisa Helmanis and Elisabeth Wilson for their contributions to this book.

First published in 2006 by
The Infinite Ideas Company Limited
36 St Giles
Oxford, OX1 3LD
United Kingdom
www.infideas.com

Reprinted 2007

A CIP catalogue record for this book is available from the British Library
ISBN 978-1-904902-30-0

Brand and product names are trademarks or registered trademarks of their respective owners.

Designed and typeset by Baseline Arts Ltd, Oxford
Printed in China

Brilliant ideas

Introduction

Who would have thought that something as
simple and natural as meeting and keeping a
partner would need a manual? After all, it's easy.
Don't your eyes just meet across a crowded room,
then you make idle chatter and impress each other with your witty
repartee, and the next thing you know it's all mini-breaks, expensive
dinners with flattering low lighting and happily ever after? Right?

Wrong. Our expectations of love, romance and sex have altered
massively since only a generation ago: now statistics show that
almost half of all marriages end in divorce. We're all working longer
hours, and add to that the high cost of living, and – well, you get
the picture. Romance gets moved to the back burner. So how do
you avoid becoming a statistic? Hopefully the tips in this book will
go a long way to helping you.

If you're in a relationship, or trying to find your mate, this book's for
you. You don't have to be married, straight, middle aged or old. You
can be in an age gap relationship, come from different backgrounds
and cultures, classes, clans or castes, it doesn't matter. Nor do you
have to wait until you and your relationship have become jaded and
tired before trying these brilliant ideas. On the contrary, the earlier
you sit down and think about your evolving life together the better.

We make no promises about stopping arguments forever, or guarantee that you'll never feel angry with each other again. This is real life. We are here to promote possibilities, not pipe dreams. Forget rules, you need ideas.

Here are 52 Brilliant Little Ideas that you can use to invigorate your love life. So what are you waiting for?

1. Learn from the masters

Everyone knows someone who is an incredible flirt – now it's your turn.

Rather than make a voodoo doll of the office flirt, watch and learn: the good and the bad.

Most women with these skills often seem transparent to other women; they seem to turn on the charm unashamedly and suck up to a man's ego without a second thought. Well: newsflash – men don't care. Flirting also doesn't have to be about sex. It can just be about remembering to look up, crack a smile and not take everything so seriously. Keep things light; it's a great way to stop every date you do have from seeming like a full-scale interview.

Here's an idea for you...

Look at the people who make you feel good and consider which of their qualities you like. Maybe your grandmother is a very calming person to be around because she is a great listener. Maybe your best friend is brilliant at coming up with exciting plans and making things happen. Your brother might always know how to put nervous people at ease... think about how you can adopt these easy ways of being, and look for similar traits in yourself.

Defining idea...

'The mysterious is always attractive.
People will always follow a veil.'
English writer and cleric BEDE JARRETT,
from *The House of Gold*

Most good flirts have a few skills in common. Firstly, they smile a lot and keep things upbeat, a quality that draws people whether they are friends or colleagues. Secondly, they ask questions and remember details. And thirdly, they often use physical contact – a great way of making people know that you are comfortable with the idea of being in their body space: or of having them in yours.

Modify the office flirt's tactics. Maybe you can emulate the way she remembers everyone's name or gets involved with after-work activities. It's about knowing that you might need to sharpen up your skills consciously. You can use what she does wrong to help guide you: maybe her whole conversation is about the other person, which is a great way to get attention but isn't going to help move things on to the next stage. Maybe the neckline of her blouse ends around her waistband; also not a winner with every guy in town. The wise girl looks for lessons everywhere...

This is why you also need to think about how you already put yourself out there. Are you always coming up with wisecracks or reminding men you meet how smart you are? Do you find yourself joking about, like you did with your male friends at college or your ex-boyfriend? Whilst this might be a great place to *get to* with a partner, it's not necessarily ideal when you first meet someone. Revealing yourself as you get to know one another is a much better way of allowing space for both of you to get comfortable.

2. Facing the facts

When it comes to romance, we all are masters in the art of deception – with others and with ourselves.

However, the key skill to learn when mastering the art of dating is the art of truth. You will find yourself suffering unnecessarily during the whole dating process if you cannot face a few facts (and hide some). Rather than crumbling into a heap of Kleenex when a guy tells you he isn't sure where it's going, and begging him to tell you why all men hate you, give a light hearted shrug and agree (even if you had already mentally picked out the curtains for your love nest). If he is simply testing you, he'll make the effort to get things back on track; if he really means it he has done you both a favour by nipping it in the bud and letting you leave with your dignity to keep you warm.

Having said that, men also are quite easy to work out; any of the serious relationships I have had began with the man calling when he

Here's an idea for you...

If you can't make up your mind about someone, try writing it all down as a story, using other characters to play your parts. When we hear tales about other people, their mistakes or self-delusion seem obvious, but our own blind spots are impossible to see. Sometimes we try and make the facts fit our desires rather than face up to them. Seeing things in black and white is often a good way of getting a more objective perspective.

said he would (the next day). Men aren't that complex. If they want you, they will find you. Which brings us on to...

If it has taken him more than around five days to call, then one of the following statements is probably true:

■ He isn't that into you, but wants some entertainment.
■ He has a girlfriend and couldn't get to the phone till she went off to visit her mum.
■ He thinks he is a player, and someone told him playing hard to get would drive you insane. (Note: this is also sometimes known as mental abuse.) He is incapable/not ready/frightened of a relationship.
■ He genuinely lost your number and has had to track you down through Interpol, so desperate was he to see you.

Of course, you may feel the need to see him again to work out which one of the above is at play. And if it's any of them, bar Interpol, make sure you attend the date with running shoes on. Because if it is any of the above, you are better off facing a slightly unpleasant truth with a side order of disappointment, which may take a day to get over, than wait a few months down the line till your confidence and belief in men have both taken a beating.

3. Why men love bitches

...and lovely women put up with creeps.

Nice girls (and chaps) come last

The problem for women, is that from the word go we are brought up to believe that compromising, putting others first and being amiable will be the key to popularity and appreciation. Fast forward about twenty-five years to kitchen tables and listen to the repeated refrain of women telling their best friends 'I'm so taken for granted, he treats me like his mother!' Well, that's because you act like it. Men are simple creatures; if you wash his socks, cook his meals and nod passively at his boring stories it's not going to take

Here's an idea for you...

Try saying no in all kinds of situations and see how it feels. Asked to do overtime you don't want to do or babysit a friend's kids? Say no with a smile and don't be tempted to explain – it's a favour they are requiring, not something you have to justify not doing. Be prepared for people to be angry or unreasonable, but remind yourself that those are their emotions and not yours. Once you get into the swing of drawing up boundaries you'll find it easier to stand your ground with a man you really like.

Defining idea...

'The thing women have got to learn is that nobody gives you power. You just take it.'
ROSEANNE BARR, US comedian and actress

too long before he confuses the two of you. Some men, too, behave the same way towards their partner. A man like this needs some bitchiness. The bitch will do these things but will also make sure – as her partner would – that it takes effort and that he or she expects appreciation in exchange for doing them.

Tell him straight

The key quality a bitch needs to adopt in practice is the ability to say no. If you don't want to do something, don't go and do it and then seethe in quiet resentment. It makes you feel uncomfortable and him want to avoid you like the plague. So just get it out.

Something many women fear is being regarded as high maintenance – but does anyone really want to be regarded as low maintenance? If you are clear about your needs and communicate them in a pleasant, unemotional way you stand a better chance of getting what you want. Saying 'Seven is too early to meet this evening for me, eight is better,' will let him know that you have a life and are not so desperate for attention that you will drop everything for his. You might see missing your lunch hour so you can finish your work early and make the date on time as being helpful, but he will see it as being needy. And the more he pulls away the more tempting it is to try and please him. Not a great power balance to set up in the early days.

4. Message in a bottle

Alcohol, the great lifter of spirits, calmer of nerves and friend of the good times. If only that was all it did…

While alcohol has its virtues, it can also cause a whole big heap of trouble. Alcohol affects the part of the brain that deals with inhibition, which won't surprise anyone who has found themselves on top of a table shaking their booty in only a pair of wellies and a badly fitting nurse's outfit on New Year's Eve (just me, then?). So while alcohol may make it possible for you to say a full sentence without stuttering when you're on a date, it may also mean that the sentence is a rather intimate list of all the embarrassing men you've ever slept with. Might seem funny at the time, less so when the dawn approaches and the vodka and tonic wears off. And remember, 55% of communication is non-verbal so think of all the subtleties you'll miss if you are hammered the whole time.

Here's an idea for you…

If you are unsure about a potential date, suggest something that doesn't involve night-time pursuits and see how you get on. You may have a flirty thing going on in a darkened bar but be unable to sustain a daytime chat. If it's right, then you will get the chance to find out some more personal things about each other. (And you'll make sure you still fancy him in daylight.)

19

Defining idea...

'One reason I don't drink is that I want to know when I am having a good time.'
NANCY ASTOR, politician and first woman MP in Britain

When you start to feel like your judgement is going, get a cab. If you like each other you can get together again; if not you will be glad you woke up in your own bed (alone). And if it is just some nice casual maintenance sex you are after, wouldn't it be better to be able to remember it?

There are a few great tricks to make sure that you don't end up drinking yourself into a stupor on your date. Firstly, make sure that you order water as well as wine with dinner and take alternate sips. This will help with your hangover as well as your clarity. Secondly, if you are meeting for cocktails, resist the urge to order a martini and go for something a little more sedate; a longer drink, mixed with fruit juice or soda, can pack a punch but also keep you this side of bursting into Cole Porter classics. If you are going speed dating or to a party, then make sure that you don't arrive too early, otherwise you are bound to start drinking to calm your nerves.

Safety is an issue you can't ignore. In the first place, the more you drink, the more risks you take. Secondly, if your date seems intent on filling your glass, alarm bells should be ringing. Of course, he may just be trying to keep things convivial but make sure that you pace yourself despite his efforts.

5. Money

Modern dating's a confusing world, not least when it comes to the sticky question of who pays.

So, as well as the old-fashioned rules about who asks who out, we also have the thorny issue of who picks up the bill...As a rule of thumb, whoever asks for the date should be the one to pay. However, money is not neutral and you need to think about what kind of message you are sending out when you make your decision.

Many men feel uncomfortable if a woman wants to pay; it's their last vestige of masculinity when it comes to feeling like a provider (don't laugh, it's an important part of a normal man's identity).

However, you may have fallen for a fledgling photographer who has yet to make any money, while you are riding high on your expense account. So try a picnic in the park or trips to a gallery that he can stump up for, or he will get tired of

Here's an idea for you...

Play the credit card shuffle. Sometimes on a date you may feel that it is entirely appropriate to pay half, or all, of the bill. Maybe you asked him out, or the date was so wrong for you that you want to leave without any pressure to see him again. One way of getting around the thorny issue of arguing over who pays for what is to catch the maitre'd on your way to the toilet and give him your card directly.

Defining idea...

'A wise man should have money in his head, but not in his heart.'
JONATHAN SWIFT

being the poor relation and move on. There is no denying that money is power and must be handled with care to stop it causing rifts.

Talking about money is really difficult for most people, it is an emotional issue and cited as one of the key issues in relationship breakdowns. Getting these thorny issues upfront could save you both a lot of hurt later.

So what is your own feeling about money and men? Money is often a great way of working out where you are at in many ways. Firstly, if you are a spender with credit cards mounting up all over the shop, you may be looking for someone to bail you out: not exactly the most romantic way to find a soulmate. Alternatively, you may have your chequebook tightly balanced and be unwilling to hook up with a guy who has debts; prudence is always a good thing but with things like student loans and stag nights being held in expensive locations, you might easily meet someone with problems. Money isn't a neutral issue so it is unlikely that your approach to it will be, either. Think about how it informs your emotional decisions.

6. Live sexy

Picture the scene: you are having lunch by yourself in a quiet café; you look up and see two atractive men at nearby tables.

Both are nice looking and have good bodies, and both keep looking at you… The first, with unkempt hair, has hunched shoulders and looks furtive. The second sits back in the chair and waits for you to look up before giving you a wide smile and then looking back to his menu. Which one appeals?

Of course you know nothing about either of them, but the person who seems in a happy, self-possessed place is always going to be more of a draw than anybody who looks like they need to be put through a spin cycle on extra hot. And it's not all about body language; it's about the fact that we would all like to be with someone who can enrich our lives rather than drain them.

So here's a guide to making your life utterly desirable. Being wanted is always much more attractive than being needed.

Here's an idea for you…

A common complaint from women is that men stop surprising them or whisking them away for treats and fancy weekends, but why shouldn't they expect the same in return? Keep coming up with new ideas for things for you both to try (skiing, badminton, naked horse-trekking in Peru…).

23

- Act like you know your own worth, even when you feel at a low ebb. This usually means turning off the self-deprecating drivel ('Oh no, I'm only the CEO because no one else wanted the job...').
- Friends are an essential part of a healthy life. Having mates also lets potential lovers know that you are socially adept, and are able to ask others for support rather than relying on them. No one wants a twenty-four-hour limpet relying on them for constant love and stimulus, unless they are a rock. Or just plain freaky.
- Understanding money and how to make the most of it is a very attractive quality in another person. It will give you a great sense of well-being and security too: what's not to love?
- Take some pride in your environment and see its knock-on effect on everything you do, from arriving to work early because you can actually find the matching parts of a suit or just being happy to spend time on your own because you can curl up in your nice comfy bedroom with some tea and the newspapers.
- Have weekends away with friends, girls' nights only and keep up your yoga class; these were all part of the reason he was interested in you in the first place (especially the yoga positions) so give them up now and you may both be left wondering what happened to the old, interesting you.

Defining idea...

'I was always looking outside myself for strength and confidence, but it comes from within. It is there all the time.'
ANNA FREUD, Austrian psychoanalyst and psychologist

7. Make anyone want you

Die-hard romantics may want to look away now. Unless they really want to hook someone special...

Using a few tricks to get someone interested isn't just a cynical ploy. Real love will follow if it's right.

We all have a physical 'type' that we may respond to, but studies show that we also need to feel that we must have something in common with that person. This is why you might find people who dress similarly drawn to each other; there's an element of tribal recognition (yes, even amongst accountants). It makes us imagine that we may have shared values and interests.

Mirroring is a technique that has

Here's an idea for you...

To make the object of your affections start to feel that there may be something more between you than he had realised, hold his gaze. When you have to turn to talk to another person, make sure you hold his look a beat longer than normal and then drag your eyes reluctantly away. Even though you are doing the staring, you are simulating the actions of two people in love, and you will at least have him wondering.

Defining idea...

'Imagination is the beginning of creation. You imagine what you desire, you will what you imagine and at last you create what you will.'
GEORGE BERNARD SHAW

essential to their happiness. The great news is that if you are looking to make an impact on someone, you can cheat this closeness and use it to get their attention. Good flirting uses this technique from the very start, in the form of sexy body language; touching your face if they touch theirs, leaning forward if they do... it seems to be a natural instinct that we can lose as relationships evolve and we get defensive. If you're feeling defensive in the first place, of course, you probably won't do this – so make a deliberate effort.

Repeat back ideas or phrases that they use, or make comments such as 'I can understand why you feel frustrated' or 'I really sympathise with that'. This will make them feel as if you both share a common bond and world view, something essential to falling in love.

There is a difference between mirroring someone's behaviour and becoming a strange, puppet-like version of them. You can still disagree with them and take a different stance on things, but allow someone to feel understood before you get into that sticky place where you disagree (which we are all bound to do at times). If you have been together for a little while, and feel that things quickly seem to jump to a state of friction between the two of you, then try getting back to a place of complicity by employing this technique.

8. And what do you do?

Upgrade your small talk and a better grade romance becomes a lot more likely.

In the film *White Mischief* Charles Dance clocks Great Scacchi as they walk down the stairs. There is an obvious magnetism between them. At the bottom of the stairs he turns to her and says, "Are you going to tell your husband, or shall I?"

OK, so that's a film. But it certainly beats, "What do you do?" in the first line stakes. So what are the other options? Well, instead of being bored to death by yet another conversation about commuting or childcare, suggest something you're interested in and most other people are, too. Sex, if it's the right sort of environment. Travel or scandal if you want to be a mite more sedate. Conversation is a little bit like sport, you will play to the level you are in. If someone is deadly dull, you're more likely to be so yourself and dull is NOT sexy. Either walk away from them or try to change the subject matter. Most

Here's an idea for you

Make an effort to be interesting. If you don't do, read, see or experience anything, you're not going to have much to talk about. So try to stay well-informed and alert, it's much more attractive than ignorant.

Defining idea

'Talking and eloquence are not the same: to speak, and to speak well, are two things.'
BEN JONSON, 17th century dramatist and wit

people are just as keen as you are to enjoy life. They will also want to sparkle and a good conversation will help them do that. So instead of coming out with something that people expect you to say, dare to be different and try something charming or even slightly eccentric.

Most people like to talk about themselves and have something interesting to say, even if it's not immediately apparent. In other words, you need to bring this something interesting out of them and use the time with them to bring out their best side.

A good answer to the question, 'How old are you?' is, 'About your age'. This totally floors people and also means you can avoid telling them. Adopt this attitude when people try to make dull conversation – playful and just a little bit off the wall to keep them on their toes.

Of course, some days the original one-liners will just flow. On others you'll feel totally stuck and unable even to tell someone what time it is. Concentrate a bit harder to come across as sexy and amusing. Make an effort; once you start entertaining yourself your mood will change.

9. Work it

A useful skill in promoting romance is the ability to look sensual after a hard day at work.

Start your preparation. The night before. Go to bed early, having had a long bath and done any essential grooming such as leg waxing, manicure, eyebrow plucking...

Next morning, have a shower, wash your hair and prepare yourself as you normally would for a day at work. The key is in what you take with you to work. I am guessing you will have at least an hour between leaving work and the date. This time needs to be used to give you that 'just left the bathroom' look and feel. To achieve this you will have to bring to the office make-up remover, face moisturiser, toothbrush, hairbrush, scent, deodorant, new underwear, tights/stockings and a change of clothes. If you don't feel like lugging a whole new wardrobe to work with you you can cut out the full change of clothes and just take another shirt or top with you – the

Here's an idea for you

Take another pair of shoes to the office to change into for the evening. There's nothing quite as refreshing as taking off shoes you have been running around in all day. You should also wash your feet if you possibly can, before changing shoes. If you're a bloke you might want to think about at least bringing another pair of socks

Defining idea

'Be prepared.'
Motto for the Scout Association

right top can transform office wear to evening wear. Some little extras could include a product that promises to brighten up your face like a beauty flash balm – most make-up companies do one (but be sure to apply make-up straight away afterwards or it flakes).

Once you have finished your high-powered day, lock yourself in the loo. If the one at the office isn't very nice then be bold: walk to the nearest luxury hotel and march into theirs. If you walk in looking confident people rarely question you.

Once in a bathroom, remove day make-up and immediately apply your moisturiser. Then wash under your arms; if you can, also wash your feet. Then put to good use all the kit you've brought with you.

Now for your psyche; you need to shake away the office from your brain as well as your body. Stand up straight, reach your arms above your head and then breathe out as you reach for your toes. Breathe in once you're down there and clasp your ankles. Slowly breathe in as you bend your knees and breathe out as you straighten them, edging closer to the floor with each breath. Repeat this ten times.

10. In the mood

If you're in the mood for love, or more to the point if you're not, music can enhance or change your feelings in a heartbeat.

"If music be the food of love, play on", said the playwright. And since time began music has been a great aphrodisiac. What music do you choose to set the mood? Classical music is classy and passionate. A most seductive piece of operatic music is the aria from *Don Giovanni* where he seduces Elvira. It has a flow and a pace that makes you want to fall into bed with the Don yourself. He tells her to give him her hand and explains how she will say yes. She protests that she feels sorry for her fiancé. The Don tells her he will change her life. But be careful, if you end up smooching to this you might get a rude awakening when the earth opens and Hell claims the evil seducer at the end, rather loudly. A more relaxing option might be Mozart's Clarinet Concerto. It is one of the most perfect pieces of music ever written; flowing, seductive, entrancing. Just listen to it and tell me it doesn't move you. You might recognise it as the tune Robert Redford and Meryl Streep danced to on the terrace in *Out of*

Here's an idea for you

If you're able to, seduce your partner with some music of your own. It's never too late to learn to play the piano or guitar – think how impressed your amour will be when they find out you learned their favourite song or piece of music just for them.

Defining idea

'If music be the food of love, play on;
Give me excess of it, that, surfeiting,
The appetite may sicken, and so die.'
WILLIAM SHAKESPEARE, Twelfth Night

Africa. Opera is a great aphrodisiac when done well. I remember standing through a whole performance of *Eugene Onegin* at Glyndebourne once and falling desperately in love with my date, even though he couldn't afford seats.

You could always invite your partner to dance, not necessarily to Mozart, but how about some slow and sexy blues music? Don't be self-conscious about it, just dim the lights, move the furniture out of the way, put on your favourite tune and go for it. Better still strip (or strip them) to something seductive. If you find it too embarrassing to strip and get all self conscious try loosening your inhibitions with a drink beforehand. But not too much, there's nothing as ungainly as a drunk stripper falling over her stilettos as she tries to ease off a stocking. Second tip, dim the lights or turn them off and go for candles instead. Final tip, let the mood and the music relax and seduce you. Remember that the key to being sexy is confidence. You know you can do it. Get in touch with your inner tramp.

11. Enduring allure

What can you do to rekindle the sexiness and intensity you experienced at the start of your relationship?

If you are married or living with someone and have children, finding the time to rediscover each other is not always easy. If you possibly can then go away together alone at least once every three months or so. It's not just the fact of being alone that's important, it's being away from all the chores and worries of home. Some couples also find that making a date with each other once a week helps to keep the relationship fires burning. It's a good idea if you find it hard to prioritise each other. Decide to leave work early and meet for a drink on your way home, or meet for lunch. Or make a date to meet in the bath on Thursday night when the kids are in bed..

Try to think of sex as a priority and make time for it. Slip into something sexy and buy your loved one a little gift and put every effort into seducing your partner instead. What could be more important than that?

Here's an idea for you

One evening sit down and reminisce. Go through your first date, what you wore, what you did, where you had sex. Talk about all the things that first attracted you to each other. Was it the way he talked, something he said? Was it a certain skirt she wore, the way she flicked her hair? This should bring back happy memories and rekindle lustful thoughts.

Defining idea

'Passion always goes, and boredom stays.'
COCO CHANEL

Make sure you take time to relax – you're going to find it very hard to get in the mood if you're still stressed from today or worrying about tomorrow. Add spark to your life by thinking of each day as a day filled with sexy opportunities. For example, don't just think of the bathroom as a place to shave or shower but a place to rekindle your romance.

Being sexy is of course not just about looking good. Some friends of mine recently got divorced. The husband has his own business, the wife didn't work. "I just lost respect for her," he told me. "I couldn't bear to see her wasting time and achieving nothing. She seemed to have no ambition whatsoever. In the end she also had nothing to talk about, apart from what to eat or what the kids had done at school." There are those among us who want nothing more than the luxury of staying at home and raising our children, which is great as long as you don't forget that when you got married you were an interesting person in your own right and you need to ensure you stay that way.

12. No place like home

Dates are great but the real romance happens at home.

Even if you're living together you should regularly create a sexy environment at home to enjoy. It's a lot cheaper than going out, and you can get naked a lot quicker. If you are married with children you need to get them out of the house for the evening before you start on the rest. Send them to stay with their friends overnight (which they'll love) or with a willing relative or neighbour.

Once you are alone use the time wisely and don't waste it poring over those bills and bank statements you never get round to looking at. Preparation is key. It's great fun preparing for a home date, and very easy.

Music is the first thing to organise. Whatever you chose, if you're trying to create a romantic environment, it should be something mellow. Next

Here's an idea for you

Why not create your own love nest? Buy sumptuous new bed linen – it's really worth investing in Egyptian cotton sheets, duvet covers and pillow cases. Light the room with scented candles, draw the curtains and spend the day there with your lover and a bottle of champagne. Don't forget to take the phone off the hook.

Defining idea

'Home is where the heart is.'
Late 19th century proverb

look at the lighting. Invariably your everyday lighting will be too bright. You can tone it down by turning off the main lights and draping material over the lamps, or turning off all electrical lighting and just using candles – magical. (But just make sure you don't inadvertently create any fire hazards). Floating candles are incredibly romantic and create a flattering and sensual light.

Make sure the room smells sensual and eliminate any unpleasant odours by burning some fragranced oils for a few minutes. This will give you a much more subtle and natural aroma than you would get by spraying air freshener.

Food is going to play a large part in your sexy evening in. Pick on things you can feed each other, smear on one another or generally get dirty with. Things you can eat with your fingers work well. Artichokes with melted butter, strawberries and whipped cream, grapes (seedless if possible, spitting out seeds is not a good look). Pink champagne is especially effective. There is something incredibly sexy and decadent about it. Drink it in delicate glasses or straight from the bottle and serve with strawberries – heaven.

Why not settle down together to a sexy DVD? Pick one of your old favourites or go for something unknown with a sexy element to inspire and titillate you. What comes next is entirely up to you.

13. The art of sexy travel

You'd be surprised what a difference getting there in style makes to how you feel once you arrive.

There are some essential tips you need to follow if you don't want to arrive on your romantic weekend away looking like something the cat dragged in and feeling even worse. Flying wreaks havoc with your whole body. You get dehydrated, tired and arrive looking pasty and ill. There are several ways to lessen the pain.

If you are on a long-haul flight and the lights are out, put on a moisturising face pack for the night. In the morning, wash it off and put on a moisturising serum to brighten your face up. Take lots of hand cream and some of your favourite scent to spray on when you land. Don't forget your hairbrush and breath freshener too. If you're on the flight overnight

Here's an idea for you

Any little testers you get you should save for when you are travelling. That way you will always have a good moisturiser or face pack to hand. Any time you see good quality shampoo in travel sizes snap it up. Unless you're staying somewhere really expensive where they've supplied luxurious free products hotel shampoo is just not an option. It leaves your hair lacking condition and feeling like it's been washed in nail polish remover.

Defining idea

'For my part, I travel not to go
anywhere, but to go. I travel for
travel's sake. The great affair is to
move.'
ROBERT LOUIS STEVENSON

then changing your underwear just before you land as well as your top will make you feel fresher. And remember not to succumb to the temptations of that glass of wine or gin and tonic (no matter how bored you get). Flying dehydrates you and alcohol makes it worse. Try to eat healthily, even if it means going on board with your own picnic. And remember, linen is not a good option when travelling; you will arrive looking like you need a good iron.

The stress of air travel can take a toll on your appearance too so try to stay zen. Think of this time you have to yourself as a gift and use it to listen to music, read or plan your next romantic move. Don't flap about getting cross or grumpy if there are delays or complications. These things are beyond our control, there's no point fighting them. Train travel is often a lot more relaxing, so if it's a relatively short journey why not avoid the airport all together?

Driving can also be a good way to get there. For the ultimate sexy statement hire a convertible. To avoid arriving looking like you've been dragged there wear a headscarf and some sunglasses.

Now there should be no excuse for arriving at your desination looking anything other than sexy and serene.

14. The write stuff

Expressing yourself in the written word helps you keep in touch with a loved one when you're away, and can be extremely sexy.

After our first date, my husband sent me a postcard. I can't remember what the picture was but his handwriting was so beautiful I fell in love on the spot. There is no doubt the power of the written word is huge. In the past whole relationships were conducted via letters.

Now that we live in the age of emails and mobile phones, the simple old letter doesn't really figure much. But it's amazing how romantic it is. Next time you're away from your loved one, try writing them a letter, telling them how much you miss them and describing what you would like to be doing if you were with them. The fact that someone has made the effort to write you a letter in this age of rapid communications is

Here's an idea for you

If your handwriting is appallingly bad (like mine) then try to improve it. The first thing to do is to find a pen you like to write with. Then find some handwriting you like the look of and would like to imitate. Slow your writing down. Develop a test sentence that you write every day at the top of a page. Compare and contrast to see what progress you have made

Defining idea

'Words are, of course, the most
powerful drug used by mankind.'
RUDYARD KIPLING

pretty sexy in itself. Just say what
you want. You may not think it's
important but your loved one will.
Imagine he or she is standing in
front of you and say what comes
into your head. But thoughts about
them will naturally interest them most. If you're planning a sexy
letter use beautiful paper and, women, spray a little of your
favourite scent on it to remind him of you.

Emails are a great way to keep in touch. You can flirt in emails as the
exchange is almost immediate, like a conversation. Send your loved
one a romantic email just to say you miss them – even if you're
going to see them that night.

The recent divorce between Jennifer Aniston and Brad Pitt has been
attributed in part to the fact that she caught him having telephone
sex with Angelina Jolie. You would think he might have thought
about using a mobile phone and gone down to the bottom of the
garden. Telephone sex is a great way to talk your lover through how
much you're missing them and what you'd like to do with them. It
is guaranteed to keep the sparks flying while you're away. You'll
both be looking forward to the reunion more than ever.

15. Surprise!

Monotony kills relationships. Time to reinvigorate yourself with something completely different.

Use a little imagination to spice up your everyday life and create romantic situations where you normally wouldn't.

For example, your alarm goes off at 7am, you get up, have a shower, eat something, trudge down to the underground or the bus in the pouring rain and go to work. This happens most days. But some days, something different will break the monotony: a busker playing your favourite song, a story in the newspaper that makes you laugh, a brief glance from a fellow-commuter that sets something off in the depths of your half-asleep psyche. But to notice these things you have to be receptive and ready for them.

Try to treat each day as an adventure. It's a terrible old cliché but live each day as if it were your last. Instead of thinking "God this is dreadful, I hate this commute" think "I wonder what or who is waiting around the corner?" Even if you're not so optimistic that anything remotely exciting awaits you on the 7.47 take something exciting with you like a novel full of steamy sex and adventure – it will at least get the imagination of your fellow commuters going.

Here's an idea for you

Surprise him by offering to wash his car, wearing a short skirt and stockings and suspenders. The neighbours will be eternally grateful too. (Men, adapt this idea.) Use your imagination to surprise people, including yourself!

Adopt the same approach in your relationship. If there is a choice of what to do at the weekend, always go for the most eccentric one. Things like ice skating or a picnic in a boat work better than a classic dinner out.

For your girlfriend's next birthday how about booking her a day at a fabulous spa with one of her friends? If she's more practical then what about a fabulous cookery course? There are literally hundreds advertised on the internet, all over the world. And for your boyfriend, you really can't go wrong by giving him one of his sexual fantasies as a present (though a cookery course might work for him too). You could also offer to be his sex slave for a couple of hours. But make sure he returns the favour one day.

Think about how much it meant at the beginning that your partner had even agreed to go on a date with you. Try to recapture that feeling and hold on to it, at least for a night, once in a while. Get on a bargain flight to a city you've never visited or spend all day in bed feeding each other strawberries.

Whatever you do, increase the sexiness and excitement of being together by doing something you don't normally do.

16. A certain je ne sais quoi

The French invented romance – so what can we learn from them?

Let's start with attitude. The French are naturally confident (some would even say superior or snotty). Where this confidence comes from, no one knows, but they do wander down the Boulevards as if they own them. So you need to think French, instil yourself with inner confidence and assurance. You are sexy, let no one tell you otherwise.

Appearance is important when it comes to romance. It's much easier to feel confident and romantic if you're clean and stylish than if you're not. As a rule, French women are chic and elegant. Good make up and hair are essential if you're a woman, and you guys need to practice good grooming. The fundamental mantra for the French is 'natural but not casual'. Ladies, this means light lip glosses, subtle highlights and not much eye make

Here's an idea for you

For the French the devil is in the detail so you must not skimp on accessories. Always buy the best quality shoes, belts, jewellery and handbags you can. If you go for classic styles rather than high-fashion items they will last well – think of them as investments.

Defining idea

'*Elegance is refusal.*'
COCO CHANEL

up. Get your eyelashes curled and dyed – you'll look better first thing in the morning. Men, don't feel embarrassed about buying male beauty products; French men having been moisturising for years. Regular hair cuts, well cut clothes, and refusal to give in to middle aged spread, will do a lot to keep your partner feeling romantic.

The French tend to be slimmer than us. The key to eating like the French is moderation not deprivation. You can enjoy yourself without eating half the menu and you'll be sexier for it:

■ Order a green salad at every given opportunity (helps to fill you up but virtually calorie-free)

■ Start with a mineral water when you arrive at a drinks party – if you start knocking back the plonk as soon as you arrive you're more likely to end up a dishevelled mess than winning any hearts

■ Eat real chocolate – much more sensuous and romantic than a Mars bar

■ Go for smaller portions

■ Choose goat's cheese over other cheese wherever possible – the strong taste means you will eat less of it

■ Go for olives over nuts or crisps during the aperitif

■ Never drink alcohol once the meal is over

If you're about as French as a Lancashire hotpot, fear not, this je ne sais quoi is all about attitude. You just need to believe. If you follow the tips given in the chapter you can't fail to develop a new outlook: you'll feel like you're strolling along the Croisette in Cannes, not just Chorley High Street. Take up the language as well, that way you can seduce your lover in your new not-quite-native tongue.

17. Creating a romance lair

What does your boudoir say about you?

The chances of inpressing a partner are greatly reduced if we bring them home to reveal a stained mattress on the floor along with an unwashed duvet and a pile of pizza boxes, so apply some thought and make your bedroom beautiful.

Before we even look at the main stage (that's the bed…) we need to create a tranquil and calm haven. A bedroom, space permitting, should be purely for sleeping, romancin' and reclining. All other activities such as watching TV, playing video games (you'd be surprised) and working should be taken elsewhere.

Here's an idea for you...

The chemical that tells us we are ready to sleep, serotonin, is released as the day gets darker and tells our bodies to get sleepy. Even the red standby light on your TV can interfere with this, so leave the TV in the lounge and get effective blinds or lined curtains to keep out street lights – the effect on your quality of sleep will be dramatic. If you find waking a miserable experience, get a sunlight alarm clock that mirrors the effect of dawn, gradually waking you up and letting you wake in a better mood.

When choosing a colour to decorate your room, avoid anything over-stimulating such as bright orange or red. Restful colours such as a yellow-based white (not one based on blue, as this can look cold and hospital-like), an indulgent mocha or a sweet pale violet are all guaranteed to calm the soul. A messy bedroom will not say nice things about you so remember to keep it clean and tidy.

Good bedding last you longer, but the benefits of a good night's sleep on your general well-being and productivity can't be overstated. Natural fibres are also the best option; they regulate the body temperature, take moisture away from the skin (should your nocturnal activities make you a little hot and bothered) and last far longer than man-made fibres. The luxury version for duvets is Siberian goose down (which will last between ten and fifteen years) but any feather ranges will give great comfort (and excellent support in pillows). For

Defining idea...

'Passion makes the world go round. Love just makes it a safer place.'
ICE T, US rapper.

that boutique hotel level of luxury, look out for high thread count bed linen (never less than 200) – the finer the weave, the more gentle on the skin.

When looking to buy a bed, bear in mind that we move around sixty times a night (and that's sleeping only) and a standard double bed only gives you twenty-seven inches of sleeping width per person – less than a single bed! If you want a decent night's sleep splash out on a king-size bed; it will give you a lot more room to play with...

18. Find the hero

We know the score. You fell in love with a hero and now your relationship isn't as wonderful as when you first met.

Do you miss the good old days, when your lover treated you like the sexiest creature on earth and made you feel warm and fuzzy? In the drudgery of our daily grind, it's often far easier to look for problems than solutions. At times it might feel as if the hero or heroine you fell in love with has sneaked off, but the hero is still there, waiting in the wings to be rediscovered and nurtured back to health.

Defining idea

'I remember a lovely New Yorker cartoon, so poignant I cried. The drawing was of an obviously poor, overweight and exhausted couple sitting at their kitchen table. The husband, in his t-shirt, had not shaved. The wife had curlers in her hair. Dirty dishes and nappies hung on a makeshift clothesline strung from a pipe to the fridge. They were drinking coffee out of chipped old mugs. The caption was the man smiling at his wife, saying, "I just love the way you wrinkle your nose when you laugh".'
LEIL LOWNDES, relationship expert and author

It takes a bit of effort to root out your partner's inner hero and you might have to look quite hard. So ring-fence half an hour to yourself, grab a sheet of paper and answer the following questions:

■ Why do I love my partner?
■ What would I miss if we weren't together?

The tricky part is to then share your answers with your partner. Try making a comment like, 'I like it when you make me laugh. Nobody makes me laugh like you do.'

Everyone, your partner included, lives up or down to others' expectations. Try to avoid labelling your partner. If you think 'he's not romantic' or 'she's always late', you're less likely to notice the times when he does buy roses or when she arrives ahead of you.

Say your partner has put off hanging a picture you were both given months ago. You come home one day and notice it up. Most of us would instinctively say something along the lines of 'I'm glad that picture is finally up'. The problem with that sort of comment is that it stresses the negative and sends your partner the message that he's a bit of a procrastinator. Hardly heroic. But if you breeze in and exclaim, 'Oh that looks fantastic. I really like the way you've hung that', he'll feel like a hero inside and be more likely to act like one. It's crucial to watch your tone as well as your turn of phrase.

Here's an idea for you

Spend a day noticing and appreciating all your partner's mini heroics. Try to make at least twelve comments, like: 'I love the way that even though you've been up half the night with the baby, you still look gorgeous.' At the end of the day, spend a little time alone evaluating your partner's responses. We hope you're pleasantly surprised.

19. Take a hike

Need to clear your heads of clutter and put problems into proper perspective? Go for a walk.

It's an escape from domesticity and a chance to reconnect with the person who matters. Chances are you'll walk out with a problem and home with a solution.

Here's an idea for you

Next time you find yourself getting into an argument, why not suggest you go for a walk together to take time out and regain your composure? You might agree not to discuss the contested subject, or do so only after an interval of, say, half an hour.

Unless you live in an offshore lighthouse, there is always somewhere to walk. The sort of journey we're talking about does not need to have a specific purpose or destination, though it might involve the collection of a newspaper or be broken up by a pint in a local pub; the real reason is to have a change of environment and a change of air.

Open spaces have mind-expanding properties which help you to think more clearly; all of a sudden, difficulties become more doable and problems less problematic. Walking boosts your level of serotonin, the feel-good chemical in our brains. It also releases the body's natural opiates, endorphins, giving you a buzz. When we walk with our partners we associate feeling high with him or her.

Walks give couples a chance to talk and think. And on warm summer evenings a chance to stop and drink. And it goes without saying that a walk will make any meal eaten afterwards all the more enjoyable. If you're worried about the physical effort involved then start off with short, easygoing walks and gradually build up to longer rambles – nobody says it has to be a ten-mile hike! The increased fitness levels will improve other areas of your loving life too. If there's nowhere inspiring near you to walk then drive somewhere else and walk from there.

Going for walks, years or even decades into a relationship, may take you not only down Pineview Avenue, but down memory lane as well. Indeed, if you make the same journey, retracing forgotten steps, those old passionate feelings will probably return.

Defining idea

'I have two doctors – my left leg and my right.'
ANON

But if asked for a definitive reason for recommending walking with your partner, one word comes to mind: serendipity – the faculty of making happy and unexpected accidental discoveries. Sometimes it is what you discover in the environment: a new building site to spy on, a skip to raid, an unexpectedly lovely garden, a mis-spelled ad in a shop window. More often, the happy discovery is something one of you says, triggered by something you have seen. A walk is a journey into your partner's head and heart.

20. It's in his kiss

If you believe a kiss is just a kiss, you've been conned. If you want to recapture the closeness then pucker up.

Every teenager knows kisses are an end in themselves, not just a preliminary to sex. There's mileage in them there lips. We tend to

Here's an idea for you

Set aside at least fifteen minutes and have a no-tongues kissing session that doesn't lead anywhere else. Rub your lips together, kiss the corners of her mouth to make your partner smile and enjoy all the new and forgotten sensations.

be conscientious when it comes to countering smelly breath, reaching for mints or sprigs of parsley if we've eaten onions or garlic, but how many of us pay as much attention to the state of our lips? Call us sexist, but women tend to be better at looking after their lips than men. A daily slick of balm or flavoured gloss should keep your lips in perfect kissing condition. But avoid applying it just before going into action – slippery lips make sloppy kissers. If your lips are very chapped, try exfoliating them gently by covering them in balm and rubbing softly with a toothbrush. When you kiss, think about how you move your lips. Let them dance a little, playing with different degrees of friction and tension. Nibble, squeeze or trap your partner's bottom lip or tongue. Mess about and have fun.

As a general rule, we suggest warming up and starting slow. Changing speed mid-kiss should be like changing gear, smoothly and at appropriate times. Of course, sometimes we all like the thrill of going from 0 to 60 in three seconds, but not when we've just woken up.

Add glamour, style and fizz to a humble kiss. Take a sip of champagne, hold it in your mouth and kiss your partner. Chilled bubbles on your lips and tongue introduces an extra dimension. For a less bling-bling version, try a frozen cocktail.

One reason kissing is so popular with teenagers and older illicit lovers is the danger involved. The heady excitement that comes with the fear of being caught. Committed couples often get to a stage when this pleasure is lost and physical intimacy is taken for granted. Why not recreate early tension by having furtive kissing sessions in semi-public places, like lifts and cinemas.

Kissing's not just for lips. Rediscover your partner's body. You know about the importance of kissing places like the insides of elbows, between the shoulder blades and the backs of knees; to discover your partner's secret kiss-spots, you'll just have to ask and hope they kiss and tell.

Defining idea

'If I profane with my unworthiest hand
This holy shrine, the gentle fine is this,
My lips, two blushing pilgrims ready stand,
To smooth that rough touch with a tender kiss.'
WILLIAM SHAKESPEARE

21. Bloomin' lovely

Want your love life to blossom? Say it with flowers.

Whatever your sentiment – striking, sensual, sanguine or sexy – there's a stem out there that will say it for you. You can't go wrong with roses. Velvety crimson petals exuding the heady smell of rose. Reeks of seduction, doesn't it? Orchids, jasmine and lilies are also renowned for aphrodisiac scents.

Here's an idea for you...

If you've left it too late and all you can find is a wilted bunch at the twenty-four-hour shop all is not lost: take everything out of the wrapper and remove any ties. Pick out all the droopers and bin them. Cut off any brown or gunky bits from the remaining flowers. Better already, isn't it? Now put them in a bucket of fizzy mineral water, or still water with soluble aspirin. By the time you hand it to your beloved, it should look stunning. No guarantees for the morning after, though.

Lots of people make the mistake of thinking flowers are just for women. Rough and ready can appeal to men. Why don't you fill some empty glass jars with cut flowers? You can use coffee jars, cooking sauce containers or jam jars. Soak off the label, fill it with water and bung in some blooms. If you cram the flowers in tight, it doesn't matter what you use. Daffodils, tulips, peonies. They don't have to be shop bought. Even daisies and buttercups look fantastic. Either distribute the jars randomly around your home or group them in threes in the dining room, mantelpiece or bedside table.

Defining idea

'People from a planet without flowers would think we must be mad with joy the whole time to have the things about us.'
IRIS MURDOCH

While you're at it, is there any way you can personalise your floral gift? For example, why not give your partner a terracotta pot planted with their favourite flower seeds. On the pot you could write 'My love for you keeps growing.' Corny, but it'll do the trick.

To be really flash with flowers, you need to be au fait with the hand-tied bouquet. Just follow these six steps. It's worth the effort.

- Put the stems in a bowl of water and, using a sharp kitchen knife, remove all the side-shoots and leaves that will be underwater when the bouquet is in its vase.
- Choose one striking flower and hold it upright in your left hand (or right hand, if you are left-handed).
- Add a few flowers. Make sure that the flower head is to the left and stem is to the right. As you add flowers, twist the flowers a quarter of a turn.
- Carry on adding flowers a few at a time and twisting. Twisting makes a spiral stem so the flowers stand upright.

- When you have run out of flowers, tie with ribbon at the place where you were holding them in your left (or right) hand.
- Wrap more ribbon round the stem if you want to. You can use raffia, wire or twine instead of ribbon.

22. Present perfect

Birthdays, anniversaries, high days and holidays – what do you give the partner who's got everything?

If all your previous presents have passed their pleasure-by date, be inspired by our contemporary take on traditional tokens of affection.

Pamper with a hamper

We can't think of a present that better captures what celebrations are all about. Pamper with a hamper that reflects your partner's individual style, tastes and interests.

For example, if he's a football fan, cover a box with pictures from a football magazine and fill it with a ticket to see his team, a pair of football boots, chocolate-covered footballs or memorabilia, like a season ticket from the year he was born. Wrap it in his team colours.

If she's a keen cyclist, prepare a package of bike accessories: a map of cycle routes, a voucher for a day's tandem hire, cycling shorts, a personalised water bottle or a new D lock. Lover's a shopaholic? If you don't know her sizes, slip a voucher for her favourite shop into the handbag she's been drooling over all season. Wrap in a silk scarf and fasten with a brooch.

Here's an idea for you

Instead of one big present, try five small ones – one for each of the senses. And the perfect card? Shop bought or home made? You'll have to use your sixth sense for that – intuition.

Theme

How about giving presents according to traditional wedding anniversary themes? You don't have to be married. Use them to celebrate the anniversary of when you first met, first moved in together or first smiled at each other across a crowded train.

1st paper: books, book tokens, or hey, any paper voucher
2nd cotton: crisp, fresh, egyptian cotton bed sheets.
3rd leather: you can go any way you want with this one: a pair of fitted leather jeans, flattering pencil skirt or thigh high boots. And for the guys? Wallets are always welcome, especially if you slip something inside it.
4th linen: choices, choices: will you update bed linen, choose a gorgeous tablecloth and serve a memorable meal on it, or pledge to do all her laundry for a year?

Defining idea

'A wedding anniversary is the celebration of love, trust, partnership, tolerance and tenacity. The order varies for any given year.'
PAUL SWEENEY

5th wood: something personal (possibly hand crafted by you) will go down well – how about a small piece of furniture or a jewellery box?

6th iron: a wrought iron bed or a trouser press. What would your partner rather have? You know him better than we do.

7th copper: shiny pots or pans? Or perhaps plant a copper beech tree in the garden.

8th bronze: treat her to a fake tanning treatment, or better still, a holiday where she'll develop a real one.

9th china: a bone china dinner set. Alternatively, you could take him on a trip to the great wall.

10th aluminium: send your partner to the skies with a flying lesson.

23. Holiday romance

Use a vacation to inject a little romance into a jet-lagged love affair.

All too often, rather than being a lover's retreat, holidays stress our relationships. Perhaps it's time to do it differently.

Whatever the weather, there's a perfect trip to recharge your love batteries. Spring is a time for renewal and growth; a perfect time for a reviving tour. Discover a new city together to learn new things about each other. Make the most of soaring temperatures and hot up your relationship. Miles of sandy beaches are perfect for holding hands and strolling.

Here's an idea for you

Make your partner's eyes twinkle. We know a couple who always tell the hotel it's their anniversary. Many upgrade them to a room with a better view or bigger terrace, and even if they don't leave a complimentary magnum of champagne, they'll usually provide drinks on arrival, a bowl of fruit, flowers or a special cake.

Or how about an autumnal adventure? Pony trekking, quad biking or climbing will all leave you drenched in adrenaline, a key re-energising chemical. If your relationship's felt a bit frosty, don't suffer a winter of discontent – warm up in a winter wonderland. There's nothing like cosying up in a comfy chalet before hitting the hot tub.

'Where do you want to go this year?'
'I don't mind, where do you want to go?'
'I don't know. Why don't you choose?'

Sounds familiar? Holiday couple trouble often has roots in different expectations. It pays to establish what each of you wants. Are you

Defining idea

'If you wish to travel far and fast, travel light. Take off all your envies, jealousies, unforgiveness, selfishness, and fears.'
GLENN CLARK, founder of Camps Farthest Out

yearning for a peaceful escape or a daring adventure? Short trip or longer, more leisurely leave? Struggling to work out what you want? Think about your last holiday together. What worked well and what would you like to do differently this time? Compare your fantasy holidays and try to combine the best of both. If you're stuck, it's time to get the dice out. Write down your three top destinations each and number them one to six. Flip a coin to decide who gets to roll the dice, and…you've guessed it…the dice decides your final destination.

We suggest you agree on a holiday budget. Agreeing an upper limit for your trip, any presents, going out and souvenirs may seem excessively anal, but the bottom line is that it helps you leave money problems at home while you're away.

Plan a holiday that revolves around your partner's favourite book. If he loves *A Room with a View*, then arrange a trip around Italy. Track down restaurants, art galleries, cafés and other places mentioned. How do they measure up in real life?

24. Undercover agents

Lace or latex? Satin or silk? Your underwear is an effective relationship barometer.

At the start of relationships women tend to wear matching bras and briefs, lace body suits and slinky camisoles. And men make sure their underwear is clean. A few years down the line, we make the mistake of thinking we can get away with any old greying, fraying baggy granddad pants, because they're out of sight. No matter how long you've been together, knowing your partner is wearing underwear she looks fantastic in can give you both a little thrill. We're not saying flash your pants, but try giving him a little glimpse of your bra which has a captivating little detail like an embroidered dragonfly or sequins. Or let your partner know that under that sombre grey business suit, there's a shot of her favourite colour.

Tights are ugly. Nothing puts a damper on a relationship faster than a glimpse of flesh-coloured

Here's an idea for you...

Why not go through each other's underwear drawers and give some of the residents a new lease of life as dusters? Of course, it's hard to tell what they look like when they're lying in the drawer, so draw the curtains and get modelling.

61

Defining idea

'Brevity is the soul of lingerie.'
DOROTHY PARKER

nylon wrinkling at the crotch. So whether you want to wear fishnets, lace tops or sheer, keep him in suspense with suspenders and hold up your relationship with held up hosiery – start stocking shocking stockings.

Most women are wearing a wrong sized bra, which can be uncomfortable and unattractive. You could go and be fitted professionally in a lingerie shop, but it's much more fun to do it together at home. Here's how: get your partner to measure around your rib cage, directly under your bust. Adding five inches gives you your size. If it's an odd number, round it up to the next even one. Now the fun bit. Ask him to measure around the fullest part of your bust. And the sums: compare the two numbers. Every inch difference is a letter size. So if you're 28 inches around your rib cage (plus 5 makes 33, rounded up to 34) and 34 around your bust, you're a 34A. If you're 31 inches round your rib cage (plus 5 makes 36) and 40 inches round your bust, you're a 36D.

Underwear represents the secret and intimate side of your relationship. But the right underwear can affect the way you look and feel in your outerwear too. When you choose underwear for yourself or your partner, think about what they'll wear it under to avoid an ugly visible pantie line.

25. Stormy weather

If only relationships – and life – were all plain sailing. Here's a chart to navigate you through the choppy waters.

Some relationships books claim that arguments can be banished from your life. An outrageous claim. Arguments happen in the best households, but they don't have to end in tears, tantrums or broken china.

Arguments are part of life and love. At best, they can spur you on to change aspects of your relationship or make you notice that your partner is unhappy. At worst, serious sulking or screaming sessions drag on for days, becoming aggressive power battles, and leaving you hurt and ground down. Disagreements can actually give your relationship a boost rather than lead to a bust up if you

Here's an idea for you

The trick is to pre-empt problems before they escalate. It takes about half an hour, a bit of patience and goodwill. Let each partner have five minutes to put their point of view across. The other partner has to shut up and listen for those five minutes. Then it's their turn. Next, work together to come up with a choice of possible solutions. Discuss the pros and cons of each until you reach one you can both live with. You will both have to be prepared to compromise.

follow these rules for a good row:

■ Prevention is better than cure. If you always end up arguing about household bills, draw up a budget you both agree with.

■ Discover what you're actually arguing about. Most arguments happen because of disagreements about work, money, sex or children. If you can resolve how you both feel about these topics, you'll live in blissful harmony. Unfortunately, it takes most of us a lifetime.

■ Forget about point scoring.

■ Use words, not fists. If it gets violent, get help or get out.

■ Insults, put-downs, critical comments, sarcasm and humiliation are all below the belt.

■ Compromise. If seeing your partner's socks on the floor makes you seethe, do a deal. Bargains like 'I'll wash up if you take the rubbish out' are less likely to cause fall outs than 'You lazy tosser. Clean up your own mess or go back to your mother.'

■ When you've both calmed down, sort out the reason behind your argument. For example, if you've argued about the phone bill, find a time to talk about it.

■ Say sorry when you hurt your partner.

Defining idea

'At this present moment I have a strong urge to go over there, wrap both his legs around his neck and stick his suede shoes in his mouth. But I suppose that would only be termed a temporary solution.'
From *Sisterly Feelings* by ALAN AYCKBOURN

- Forgive your partner for hurting you and forgive yourself for being unkind.
- Make up before you go to sleep.

26. Scentsational

We'll show you how to achieve the sweet smell of relationship success by following your nose.

Educationalist Jean Jacques Rousseau called smell the 'sense of imagination'. It is the sense most closely related to memory, and learning a little about its science will score well in your relationship.

Just over 50 years ago, a group of German scientists were looking at some silkworm moths. They found that a certain chemical, which they called pheromone, made the moths very frisky. Twenty years later, and after studying 500,000 female moths, they hit the jackpot. They'd isolated a compound that made male moths beat their wings in a sexual dance. So what, you

Here's an idea for you...

Delicious food smells are welcoming and nurturing. But if, like us, you don't have time to bake every day, cheat by burning sticks of vanilla incense in the kitchen.

might well ask? Well, like moths, we also produce chemicals that arouse our partners (and other interested parties). Men's and women's pheromones smell different. Men's sweat is more acidic than women's, so male pheromones have a more musky quality than female ones. Musk, an ingredient commonly used in perfumes, is a top turn on for women. So now you know what to look out for on those aftershave and scent bottle labels. And smelling lavender, doughnuts, liquorice, oriental spice and cola can all increase blood flow to the penis. If you don't fancy putting eau de doughnut in your oil burner, you might be interested to read that essential oils cinnamon, jasmine, musk, patchouli, rose, sandalwood and vanilla are the sexiest members of the aromatherapy dynasty. They're believed to stimulate release of neurochemicals, triggering sexual responses.

Did your mum tell you to apply perfume to your wrists? Good, but other pulse points, like your navel, collarbone, behind your knees or on your ankle, often get overlooked. Match your body lotion and perfume. In fact, layering, as the beauty pros call it, is the best way of making scent last. Use perfumed shower gel or bath essence, then body lotion or talc, before spritzing with eau de parfum (that's the concentrated one) and topping up during the day with eau de toilette.

Create a super scent-sual environment by lighting scented candles all around your home. Soft light and suggestive smells will get you both into a peaceful, loving mood. As a general rule, men like pine, sandalwood and frankincense, while women often prefer rose, lemon grass or ylang ylang. But we believe rules were made to be broken, so play around and find out what chills you both out or turns you on.

27. Venn I fall in love

Stuck in a rut? Every discussion ending in an argument? Then it's time to return to the drawing board.

Ever felt stranded in your own bubble? Isolated from your partner and drifting ever further away? Don't go round in circles. Draw some overlapping ones instead.

1. Both draw two large overlapping circles. One circle represents each of you and the overlap represents things or qualities that are common to you both. This exercise can be used for or adapted to any areas of your joint life. You can use it to focus on your finances, social life, thoughts on children, pets, attitudes to parents and in-laws, careers or holidays. In each of these areas, the stuff in the

overlap of your Venn diagram is the glue that sticks you together. These might be shared values, interests or relationships with friends, but they're the things that make you both happy.

Tom

Golf, Crime Fiction and Watching Boxing.

TV especially Friends and the News. Watching Football, Cycling, Darts, Pubs and Drinking and Going to Comedy Clubs

Jerry

Clothes Shopping, Reading Chick Lit, TV Soaps and talking to Sheila on the phone.

2. Spend about fifteen to twenty minutes filling in these Venn diagrams as comprehensively as possible. You can also include names of friends you have and don't have in common, places, TV programmes, books, films, newspapers, even politics. The more wide-ranging and specific you can be the better, though you may need slightly larger circles.

Here's an idea for you...

Fighting over lack of funds? Each list your own preferences for where the money should go and see what can be moved into a central overlap section.

3. Share and compare. Time for some home truths. Some things will be self-evident while other items will need to be qualified: 'I put your mum in my bit because I like her and get on with her and you don't.'

4. Now it's time to look at the overlap and brainstorm ways of focusing on what you've got in common. If you both hate washing up, perhaps it's time to buy a dishwasher.

5. Again using words in the overlap, try to deconstruct mutual interests. What is it about darts you both find so attractive? Is it being competitive, being a member of a team, the banter in the pub, or representing the pub in other locals? This sort of questioning generates ideas for other shared interests.

Defining idea

'Studies show that similar partners have a much better chance of staying together. Similar values keep the love coals warm long after the first flames of passion have cooled.'
LEIL LOWNDES, relationships expert and author of *How to Make Anyone Fall in Love with You*

28. Jealous guy

Banishing jealous feelings is bound to revitalise your relationship. Recognise them and act.

Jealousy's a funny emotion. The object of your desire wanting you all to him or herself can be strangely seductive, for a little while. But once the glorification has worn off, relentless jealousy grates.

Here's an idea for you...

Remember, jealousy is about power and control. If your partner is jealous, chances are she controls most aspects of your life together. It's time to redress the balance. For example, if your wife usually decides where you go on your family holiday, be assertive and explain that you would like to choose this year. Maybe your boyfriend has chosen the last six cars you both own. Go to some car dealers together and show him what you are buying next.

Jealous partners make us feel like caged lovebirds: trapped and aching to fly away at the earliest opportunity. Maybe you've been censoring conversations, seeing friends less or are afraid of provoking a watchful partner into one of her rages. Jealous lovers are usually deeply insecure. But take heart. Once you understand that their possessiveness isn't a sign of your desirability but comes from a need to be loved and to control, you can tame the feral green-eyed monster.

Soon after Jack and Tina got together, she went to visit her mother in France. 'Jack phoned me three times a day,' recalls Tina. 'At first I was touched and thought he missed me. After a couple of days I realised he was checking up on me and was jealous of the good time I was having.' When Tina came home, she confronted Jack, who admitted he was afraid she would run off with a Gallic god. After she reassured him she wasn't looking elsewhere, they struck a deal. No phone calls during the day, except if there was a life-or-death emergency. Jack learned to trust Tina and his jealous feelings were checked before getting out of control.

Let's be honest. Window shopping, eye candy, whatever you want to call it – everyone looks at other people sometimes. Most of us are just discreet enough not to get caught. If you and your partner can agree on a look but don't touch rule, there isn't

any need to feel threatened. If you can go one further, and point out other people your partner will probably fancy, what relationship expert Leil Lowndes calls giving 'guilt free snacks', the green-eyed monster will turn into a green-eyed house pet. In Leil's words, 'If he has his guilt free gander, you will have a much happier goose.'

29. Flirt alert!

Make sure a little harmless office flirting doesn't turn into something more dangerous.

A frisson of safe excitement can brighten office life and casual flirting makes a mundane journey or chore a lot more enjoyable. The danger is located at home. Almost imperceptibly the passion and sparkle that once existed in your domestic life can leak away like water from a punctured paddling pool. The trick is to find ways to keep the flame of passion alight with your partner.

Here's an idea for you...

Long-term love can survive short-term crushes, as long as they're not kept secret. If there's someone you fancy, tell your partner. It isn't your girlfriend pointing out the other woman's buckteeth and hairy ankles that kills your interest, but the fact it isn't a private passion.

Working out exactly why you do anything is nigh on impossible. So you find yourself thinking obsessively about someone at work. Your 'look but don't touch' rule might not have been broken, but there are dangers. You need to ask yourself a number of difficult questions: what is it about this person that has so captivated you? Is it her youth and her ability to make you feel younger/wiser/brighter/funnier/sexier? Are things going on at home that make you feel pushed out, taken for granted, bored or boring and unheard?

Changes in circumstances can rock the boat. Promotion, a new secretary who you see more of than your wife and opportunities for foreign business trips might put previously undreamt-of temptation your way and into the equation. These are not excuses and should not be used to justify yourself to anyone, just information to help you understand what's going on.

There are times in relationships when eyes (and hands) are more likely to wander:

■ After the birth of a new baby
■ When you're raising a young family

- The 'midlife crisis'
- When the last of your children has left home
- Approaching retirement

Defining idea

'While the forbidden fruit is said to taste sweeter, it usually spoils faster.'
ABIGAIL VAN BUREN, American advice columnist

Sitting down together, anticipating difficulties and working out ways around them is a more constructive way forward.

How to avoid temptation

- Build self-esteem: people often have affairs to feel better about themselves. Pulling a new partner makes you feel successful at something and desirable again. But only in the short term.
- Face problems when they arise: affairs can be a way of avoiding trouble at home. Dealing with the root of small problems as they arise prevents a lot of bother later.
- Cultivate emotional intimacy: you both need to say how you feel to understand each other's moods and outbursts. If things feel fiery, take time out to cuddle up.

Affairs can be fun because they are furtive and clandestine. Why not have an affair with your partner? Meet in a bar and pretend not to know each other. Watch other men flirt with her, before chatting her up. Wink at him across a crowded train carriage. Have a secret rendezvous. Phone him at work and whisper a playful come-on. Or send saucy emails.

30. The hardest word

Some of us would rather face a firing squad than admit we're wrong. If the 's' word sticks in your throat, it's time to bite the bullet.

Everyone screws up sometimes. But trying to blame your partner isn't the answer. Perhaps you are afraid of losing face or looking weak. After all, saying sorry means admitting you're wrong. Perhaps you feel resentful because you always end up apologising first. It could be that it's not your fault or you don't see eye to eye. It's hard to say sorry when you don't know why your partner is angry or upset.

Here's an idea for you...

Try saying sorry next time you catch yourself hurting your partner's feelings. In your mind, rate how difficult it was out of ten, where ten is 'will the ground please open and swallow me up'. Your first couple of apologies might feel off the scale, but once you've had a bit of practice, you'll get it down to an easier two or three.

The best time to say sorry is as soon as you notice that you've hurt your partner. Now, we're not saints either, and know it's incredibly difficult to break mid-argument and offer an apology. Especially if you're winning. If you can express regret after, or even during, an argument, great. On the other hand, if you calm down a bit you won't sound sarcastic or insincere. Saying sorry is useless unless your partner knows why you're apologising. You need to acknowledge what you've done wrong. Be specific. It might make you squirm, but which of these apologies packs most punch?

'I'm sorry.'
'I'm sorry you're upset.'
'I'm sorry I upset you by calling you a lazy slag. I didn't mean it. I came home irritable and took it out on you. I know I shouldn't have said it.'
Sarcasm or a half-hearted apology, like 'You know I didn't mean it' or 'You know I'm not all bad', is worse than no apology at all because your partner will probably feel you are being disingenuous.

Apologies need to be accepted with grace and good will, rather than as ammunition for mud slinging and accusation.

Words are sometimes enough, but actions usually speak louder. Gifts can make your partner feel pressurised or even blackmailed into accepting your apology before he's ready. Far better to follow your verbal apology with action related to your transgression. If your partner's cross because you never wash up, get the rubber gloves on or buy a dishwasher. If your girlfriend's upset after finding your stash of *Horny Housewife*, cancel the subscription. Whatever you've done, there's no greater crime than apologising only to commit the same sin again.

Defining idea

'You're either part of the problem or you're part of the solution.'
ELDRIDGE CLEAVER, founder of the Black Panthers

31. Raise your pulse

Daredevil dates that make your partner's heart beat faster will make you irresistible.

Sharing a breathtaking adrenaline rush with your partner will give them the hots for you all over again.

Thirty years ago, a couple of psychologists conducted an experiment where they asked a group of guys to cross one of two bridges. The first was a scarily shaky suspension bridge far above a canyon; the other was a solid bridge just a short height over a small brook.

Here's an idea for you...

For an unbeatable combination of adrenaline and fun, why not visit a theme park? Hurtle full speed down water flume rides or corkscrewesque rollercoasters. Don't be put off by hoards of noisy schoolkids by avoiding weekends and the school holidays. Many theme parks open late one evening a week. Find out if yours does and go on a late date with a difference.

After each man crossed his allocated bridge, he was met by a beautiful researcher. She asked him to complete a short questionnaire, in which he had to categorise some fairly vague pictures of people. When he'd done this, the beautiful researcher gave the guy her phone number. 'Call me,' she said, 'if there's anything you want to ask about the study.' Guess what? The guys who crossed the wobbly bridge were much more likely to call. What's more, they found more sexy themes in the ambiguous pictures they were shown after crossing the bridge. Why? Well, crossing the suspension bridge gave them an adrenaline surge. When they saw the beautiful woman, the men misinterpreted their increased heart rates and thought they must be sexually aroused. Do something scary with your beloved, and make it work for you.

Defining idea

'*The pattern of autonomic arousal does not seem to differ from one state to another. For example, while anger makes our hearts beat faster, so does the sight of a loved one.*'
WALTER CANNON, physiologist and emotion expert

The bad news is that the converse works, too. If you and your partner are supremely bored, sooner or later she'll start to think of you as dramatically boring. So go on a different sort of date. Dare you try one of these?

Paragliding: instead of lying on the beach, go gliding. Hold on to each other tight, and when you're high above the water, whisper 'I can really feel your heart beating quickly'.

Bungee jumping: find a centre that does couple bungees, where you jump on the same cord.

Quad biking: speed junkies will love an exhilarating off-road tour across rough terrain, along mud roads, down hills and across creaks.

White water rafting: it'll build team spirit as you work together to control the raft.

And yes, we sound like your mother, but please be careful on your daredevil dates. Remember, you're aiming to raise adrenaline levels, not the mortality rate.

32. Our house

The foundations of your miscommunications may be closer to home than you think.

Is it time to clear out and cuddle up? Or should you move out and move on? We all know how it feels to see dirty dishes left in the sink again, or the bedroom floor used as a laundry basket. Our homes affect how we feel about our relationships. If all your time, energy and money are being poured into your bricks and mortar, it's not surprising your relationship needs re-cementing.

Often treasures from our past anchor us there preventing us from concentrating on what matters now. If the thought of parting with old books, music and clothes you've grown out of depresses you, at least sell, donate or throw away reminders of previous relationships.

When one partner moves into a home the other already owns or rents, it's vital to make space. Your relationship will feel a lot more equal if you go through the flat, clearing out old books and CDs, and 'rationalising' collections of whatever you own that says 'this is my house', whether it be china pigs or old issues of Computer Weekly.

Some couples work so hard climbing the property ladder that it destroys their lives and relationship. A large house, ideal for a growing family, might become a white elephant when the kids have left.

Time to move out and move on? Muse on these with your beloved:

■ What does this home stop us doing?

■ What was it that first attracted us to this home?

■ How have our needs and circumstances changed since?

■ How has the area changed: is it a better or worse place than it was?

Here's an idea for you...

Try to devote one part of your home to your relationship and romance. This will usually be the bedroom, but if you live in a microflat, sleeping on a fold-away futon, you might have to use a bit of imagination. Move the exercise bike and television, hang a couple of pictures of the two of you, a framed poem, soft lighting – whatever makes your hearts beat faster.

Defining idea

'I really do believe it: if you can live
through remodelling a home, you can
live the rest of your lives together.'
JENNIFER ANISTON, actress

- Could we convert the house
  and change its use?
- What would we miss if we
  moved?
- If we replaced this house with
  an inexpensive flat, how would
  we spend the windfall?

Perhaps the garden has become a burden rather than a joy, or the
house that was ideal for entertaining hasn't seen a dinner party in a
decade. So what could you do? Downsize, relocate, learn the
language and move to Spain? Or perhaps you want to hold on to your
family home but could use it more effectively. Taking in students
from the local uni will bring in some cash and might have the added
benefit of keeping you young and introducing you to new things.

33. April in Paris

**Long-haul lovers know mini-breaks make
a massive difference.**

Mini-breaks are a chance to live life away from
the mundane grind. Forty-eight hours to put some sparkle back and
see you through hard times. It doesn't matter whether you go to

Paris or Pontefract; it's what you do when you get there. The secret is to forget all about location and instead plan around an activity your partner will delight in.

When your chocoholic chap realises you've taken him to Belgium for a handmade truffle demonstration, or your wife realises you've travelled miles to see her favourite comedian, it all falls into place. When the world revolves around you for a couple of days, you feel understood, loved and cherished. We're not saying four poster beds, champagne and roses don't help, they're just optional extras. Think of them as garnish.

If you can keep your mini-break secret from your partner and make it a surprise, you're onto a winner. If you can't collect your partner, you could send a taxi or a mysterious email saying 'Meet me at the airport at 7pm', which will make your beloved's heart beat faster.

If money is tight, we suggest you spend most of it on your activity and scrimp on the accommodation. You can turn a grotty room in a cheap B&B into a boudoir in four simple steps.

■ If the bed sheets are nylon or chintzy, strip 'em off. Replace them with plain white cotton pillowcases and sheets.

Defining idea

'*After sitting in semi darkness for third weekend running with Daniel's hand down my bra, fiddling with my nipple as if it were some sort of worry bead, I suddenly blurted out, "Why can't we go on a mini-break? Why? Why? Why?" "That's a good idea," said Daniel mildly, "Why don't you book somewhere for next weekend? Nice country house hotel. I'll pay."*'
HELEN FIELDING, from *Bridget Jones' Diary*

- You need two roses and a jar. Put the healthier looking rose in the jar of water and put it on your partner's side of the bed. Scatter the petals of the other rose over the crisp white sheets.

- Chill a bottle of bubbly in the landlady's fridge, in your sink or by dangling it out of the window – whatever. It doesn't even have to be 'proper' champagne – any sparkling wine will do.

- Use soft lighting. A room lit by a fluorescent strip light or, worse still, a turned down television will never be a boudoir. A row of tea lights down a windowsill or in front of a mirror, on the other hand, are very effective.

34. Wonderful tonight

Give your old flame first-date butterflies with a makeover that brings out the best in both of you.

Just because he's seen your bikini line in 'relaxed' mode doesn't mean you can't still turn his head. All you need is a little application...

Many department stores offer a free personal shopper service for men and women. Be upfront. Explain that you want a look to make your long-term lover weak at the knees rather than weak at the stomach. The shopper should then bring you a selection of styles to suit your size, frame, personality and budget. It's up to you whether you love it or leave it.

There's no quicker way to change your partner's reaction from ho-

Here's an idea for you...

Wouldn't it be great if you could take the afternoon off and spend it at a spa before meeting your partner in the evening? Most of us can't do this very often, but you can achieve a similar effect in about twenty minutes. Guys, pop into an old-fashioned barber's for a really close shave. Women, befriend a department store make-up counter assistant. Say something like, 'I'm happy with my look for work, but I want to look foxier in the evenings.' You'll get a free makeover, using all the latest tricks and techniques. 'Test' some new perfume as you go out and you're set to wow him.

Defining idea

*'You have to remember that before
two hours of hair and make-up even I
don't look like Cindy Crawford.'*
CINDY CRAWFORD, modest supermodel

hum to wow than by blowing your
budget at the hairdresser. While
we're talking about hair, be a
smooth operator and get rid of any
facial hair (nose and ears too).

Get that come hither look by
plucking your eyebrows into shape. Yes, even men – eyebrows that
meet in the middle make you look like Dracula, and you know what
trouble he had in keeping a woman! If you haven't got time to do
full eye make-up, a whip of mascara can transform your look,
drawing attention to your eyes. Many metrosexual men already
know mascara also comes in clear.

Eyes may be the windows of the soul, but when you reach out to
touch your partner, how often is it with silky smooth hands rather
than ones chapped and worn by washing up, gardening or typing? A
callused caress isn't very sexy. If you usually work with your hands,
it's time to get to work on your hands. Smooth rough hands by
mixing some sea salt with some olive oil and rubbing it all over
them. A few strokes with a nail buffer means you can leave nails in
the buff, if you haven't time to polish up your act with varnish.

35. With a little help from your friends

Time to clear out your address book as you would old clothes.

If you can recognise friends and other couples who can help you re-energise, you'll get a revamped social life as well as a richer relationship. Sadly, some friends have a stake in keeping your relationship how it is. Call us callous, but they have to be jilted before you can enjoy the love life you really want.

Many friendships depend on us playing set roles: mother, office superstar or immoral wild child. When your relationship changes, these roles change too. There are also some people who seem magnetically drawn to problems and misery. One thing we've been surprised by is just how few friends want to share our good times and triumphs. It's not malice, just life.

Fill your lives with people you admire, who inspire you and who

Here's an idea for you...

Conduct an address book audit – taking a good look at the people you call friends. While you're at it, why not see if there's anyone you could get to know better? Ask them out for a double-date with their partner and take it from there. It might not work, but you'll never know until you give it your best shot.

Defining idea

'God gave us our relatives; thank God
we can choose our friends.'
**ETHEL WATTS MUMFORD, American
writer**

will support you. Your new friends
should have some of the following
qualities (if they have them all,
move in immediately):

- Couples where you like and get
  on with both partners equally.
- Couples in relationships where
  no one is the boss.
- Couples who are great listeners, who seem interested in you and
  your lives.
- Positive people who are prepared to try new things.
- People who share your sense of humour and fun.
- Couples prepared to give your joint relationship as much time
  and effort as you.
- People who are great mixers, who get on with your family and
  other friends, and who you are happy to see in any company.
- People you can talk to when you or they are unhappy about
  something.
- People who reciprocate hospitality.
- People who don't take sides in one of your fall-outs.

Banish these types:
- Snipers: people who have envious pops about your house, job,
  car, relationship, lifestyle.
- Control freaks: some couples and individuals have to
  dominate. This is bad news whether it is conversation subject

matter or where you'll eat. These sorts of choices ought to be mutual.

■ Bloodsuckers: friends who are affected with contagious forms of negativity. Spend an evening in their company and take a week to recover.

■ Sulkers: 'friends' unable to accept that you can't always drop everything and have a meal with them at two hours' notice. They'll make you feel guilty.

36. Love and marriage

Arranging your own special day gives your relationship a boost that lasts.

A marriage certificate may just be a piece of paper, but the emotional investments, legal ties and public declarations make it your most important possession. Living in sin? Marriage has a lot going for it, you know. Cohabiting comes with legal implications, like not being recognised as your partner's next of kin. Maybe you're a commitment-phobe? Already notched up one or more unsuccessful marriages? Enjoying the disapproval of parents or landlords? Get over it.

Publicly promising to stay with your partner forever profoundly changes your relationship. Making or renewing vows buttresses

Here's an idea for you...

Been married for years? Dust off the album, reminisce over the good times and then renew your vows. Like your wedding dress, some might not fit anymore. Perhaps you'll want to make some new ones, or use your own rather than the prescribed wording.

previous promises. Marriage is a chance to stop and think about what we want for our relationships and what we need to get there. Like it or not, his 'n' hers gleaming gold bands affect how others treat your relationship.

Heard that weddings are stressful and strain relationships? Not if you ignore the propaganda peddled by the wedding industry. Rushing around trying to find the last four hundred of this season's must-have sugared almond holders in pale yellow will frazzle your nerves and your partner's patience. Instead, work together to create a day as personal and individual as your relationship. Local silversmith colleges will put you in touch with centres where you can design and make wedding rings. Or get a shop-bought ring and have it inscribed with a secret or personal message. Laws governing the wedding ceremony vary from country to country, but in most places you can personalise a set script, add your own rituals to more traditional ones or go the whole hog and do the lot yourself. You may need a civil ceremony as well to cover all the legal bits.

If you think weddings are sexist claptrap, all about archaic property transfer rights and keeping money in the family, you're absolutely right! But not all weddings are, and certainly not the sort we have in mind. There's no reason why you and your partner can't cherry pick the best bits to create an unforgettable commitment ceremony. Commitment doesn't have to be legal to be powerful or life changing. Nevertheless, some couples do include legally binding arrangements, like wills or property ownership.

Defining idea

'Marriage is popular because it combines the maximum of temptation with the maximum of opportunity.'
GEORGE BERNARD SHAW

37. Special days

The occasional splurge may seem expensive, but it can re-energise you and your partner.

Sometimes your relationship needs a life-changing day. Perhaps you're both sick of the same routine? Husband having a hard time at work? Need to make your 25th valentine's day as dynamic as the first? Just moved house? Or the best reason of all: just because.

Book the best suite in a nearby hotel. Waking up in a mahogany four poster will make the most jaded couple feel like royalty. It's the perfect start to a wonderful day, one without the hassle of work, chores,

Here's an idea for you...

This evening, turn your dining area into a five-star restaurant. Prepare a handwritten menu of your partner's favourite dishes, put her kind of music on in the background, and cook as much as possible beforehand so you're not tied to the kitchen. Do something special in between courses. Play piano, read her a poem, look into her eyes and tell her what you see.

telephone or email. Use this day to do something totally different.

Arrange a series of treats that's something like this:

Top of the morning to you ma'am: You might go to the station to pick up the *Flying Scotsman*, or visit a racecourse or yachting regatta, or why not arrange a private guided tour of a favourite gallery or museum, followed by lunch?

Very good afternoon to you, Sir: Lunch is a cinch, but toasting each other over a proper champagne tea is an all-but-forgotten pleasure. Insist that the crusts are cut off sandwiches, which should be followed by fruit scones, pastries or a large wedge of sumptuous chocolate cake. Let your meal go down over a little light window shopping, stroll in an exclusive neighbourhood or browse antique arcades – whatever makes your partner tick.

Happy hour: Time for happy hour in a glam cocktail bar. Get into the groove by dressing as if for the Oscars, and order a large classy Cosmopolitan or Bellini, with two straws.

That's showbiz: Now on to a show. If she likes the cinema, go to the biggest, plushest one in town and reserve a big double seat at the back. If you go to the theatre or opera, book a box and order champagne for the interval.

Defining idea

'Love is like any other luxury. You have no right to it unless you can afford it.'
ANTHONY TROLLOPE, from *The Way We Live Now*

Finishing touches: Give your evening meal the film star treatment. Write a love letter or card and ask the waiter to hide it in your partner's menu. Present him with a small gift between the main course and dessert. And why not have flowers delivered to the restaurant after coffee? After you've eaten, go for a sunset stroll.

38. Domestic detox

Review your chores and renew your romance.

At the beginning of your relationship did you sit down and decide who was going to take out the dustbin every Wednesday evening? Vacuum the lounge? Cook Sunday dinner? Did you ever agree that one or other of you would do the bulk of the long-distance car journeys or always sort out the tickets for airline

Defining idea

'Hatred of domestic work is a natural and admirable result of civilization.'
REBECCA WEST, writer

bookings? Of course you didn't. Yet in most relationships, we find ourselves committed to being the only person doing a particular task. But why should one particular person be lumbered with changing the cat litter tray or making sure that the household doesn't run out of toilet paper and toothpaste?

Most men have discovered that cooking, especially if you don't have to do it all the time, is actually quite therapeutic. It's a great way to unwind at the end of the week or after a hard day at the office. Conversely, more and more women are having a go at DIY tasks. Better still, many couples have come to realise that cooking or even tidying up hardly feels like a chore when the two of you are tackling it together.

Here's an idea for you...

Have a mini household meeting at the start of each week. Write down all the cleaning, shopping, fetching, collecting and other errands that need to be done and share them out. We find it helps to write each partner's initials by their jobs. Put the list up somewhere prominent, like on the fridge or kitchen noticeboard. And don't mention it again during the week. There's no uglier utterance than nagging. Some people like to get their jobs out of the way and feel smug about it. Others are last-minute merchants. As long as everything gets done, who cares?

In a lot of long-term partnerships, one or other member suffers from what we call 'victim of your own success syndrome'. One partner always reads maps or does the big drives because he – sorry, but it usually is a he – is better at it than she is. Of course he is: he's put in the mileage. But if you share the job around, her second best can easily become joint equal. When a lover's self-esteem is built on being the sole role-holder, he might find it difficult to let go. When your partner has a go at what is traditionally your job, avoid being critical or sniping if at first they don't measure up – neither did you when you first started.

39. Cheap thrills

You don't have to blow a fortune to blow the cobwebs out of your relationship.

When was the last time you held hands and went walking at sunset or in the morning? Or played hide and seek? Or truth or dare? Or sardines? Time to make a list of things you've always wanted to know about your other half but never dared ask: think up some steamy forfeits and enjoy a night in with a difference. Or enjoy one of these

Here's an idea for you...

The key to lasting love may be on your doorstep. Play hometown tourists. Raid your nearest tourist office for free maps and leaflets about local attractions. Get out there to see your neighbourhood and each other in a better light.

Defining idea

'Money is what you'd get on beautifully without if only other people weren't so crazy about it.'
MARGARET CASE HARRIMAN

dates that won't break the bank.

■ Have an art house or blockbuster home cinema night. Rent the first film you watched together, make mountains of microwave popcorn and turn your sofa into the back row.

■ Eat at home but go out afterwards for desserts and coffee in a swanky restaurant. Share an ice cream sundae and let her have the whole wafer.

■ Rendezvous in an exclusive hotel. You don't need to book a room, just put on your finery and people watch in the foyer. Drinks may be pricey, so just buy one and enjoy complimentary nibbles.

■ Drive down memory lane. Window tour places that have special memories: where you went on your first date, had your first kiss, proposed, your favourite restaurant or view, wherever makes your hearts beat faster.

■ Want to add some drama to your relationship but can't afford a babysitter and dinner on top of top-price theatre tickets? Matinees are often half price, and if the kids are at school you won't need a babysitter. If evenings are your only option, university drama departments often put on cut-price performances for the public.

- Many artists and crafts people have open days and other free events in their studios. Find out through local arts schools, libraries or craft councils. Feeling inspired? Have creative evenings in: make a mosaic mirror, write a short story, paint a mural in the back garden, teach the cat to crochet…
- Serve your partner breakfast in bed with a themed twist. For a French breakfast, put on some accordion music and serve hot coffee and pain au chocolat. French maid's outfits and moustaches optional. French kisses, on the other hand, are just a serving suggestion.
- Drop in on an open mic night at a comedy club. As this is where new acts cut their teeth, you won't see any famous faces, but what a thrill to see someone before they were famous.

40. Touchy feely

When did you last reach out and touch the person you love?

Words are great, but your fingers can reach places language never can. We all need strokes, emotional and physical. The finest touching is a sensual conversation. When you next touch your partner, wait for a reply before touching further. So if you stroke her cheek, wait until she squeezes your arm before

Here's an idea for you...

Next time you see your partner, touch before speaking. If he's in the kitchen washing up, sneak up behind him, slide your hands round his tummy and cuddle up. When she comes home from work, give her a long hug instead of firing questions or filing complaints.

running your finger over her eyebrows. Between people who are attracted to each other, just brushing fingertips can send shock waves. Try making little circles with your fingertips on your partner's palm or inner elbow, or the nape of his neck. Do this at mundane times, like waiting for a bus or in the supermarket check-out queue.

Then next time your partner is waiting for a bus without you, he'll realise that it's just not as much fun as when you're there. A cunning piece of prestidigitation.

Hugs

We use hugs to express many different things: therapist and relationship guru Virginia Satir believes we all need four hugs a day for survival, eight hugs a day for maintenance and twelve hugs a day for growth. There are three types of hug, but only one hug hits the spot.

The quickie: A quick grab and let go, which may be punctuated by a couple of air kisses and 'mwah, mwah' noises.

The A-frame: Huggers interlock arms and may touch shoulders, but there's no physical contact any lower down.

The full body: Wrap your arms around each other, touching from the tops of your heads down to your toes, and bump tummies in the middle. Breathe together, snuggle and sigh. This one's the real deal.

The science bit

When non-sexual touch is neglected, we become belligerent and dejected. But why does touch make us feel so good? After prolonged touching, the hypothalamic area of the brain, which controls the fight or flight response, slows down and your body's natural euphoria-inducing chemicals – endorphins – soar, while the stress hormone cortisol dips. Massage has extra benefits as it promotes deep muscle relaxation. Neck massage has been shown to reduce depression, improve alertness and help people sleep more soundly. When you're being touched by your beloved, your mind associates all these good feelings with them, leaving you feeling loved up and secure. If you're going through a difficult time, try to keep a hand or another part of your body in contact with your beloved. It will help you feel united.

Defining idea

'Touch is important for survival itself. We're meant to be touched. It's part of our inherent genetic development.'
ELLIOT GREENE, past president of the American Massage Therapy Association

41. Getting it right

How do you get your lover to love you the way you want to be loved?

Just because you've been together forever, doesn't mean you press each other's buttons absolutely perfectly. Yet the man or woman who can tell their lover that they want to be touched differently from the way they've been touched a million times before is pretty rare. There are ways to ask without embarrassing yourself and mortifying your lover. Here's how to get your lover to do something differently when they think they've been getting it right for years.

The wrong way

Using phrases starting with 'Why don't you…', 'You never…' or 'That doesn't…' will cause offence and your partner will get defensive. Moreover, whining is deeply unattractive.

Here's an idea for you...

Always find something positive to say, but don't praise what's bad. Pretending to enjoy what you don't enjoy is what's got you in this mess in the first place!

The right way

Step 1: Praise, praise, praise – your new resolution: From now on, you're going to be an appreciative lover. You're going to praise your lover's performance every chance you get and using every way you can think of. This will create a 'win–win' situation. Be especially appreciative during sex. Do it with body language. Do it loudly. Spell it out: 'I love everything you do in bed', 'You're just so sexy', 'No one's ever done that to me the way that you do'. They should finish every session assured that you're blissfully happy. If they get it wrong or if they don't want to go through with it, they've nothing to lose because they know just how much you value them. Your 'win' is that besides being a lovely person you're also gearing them up for moving your sex life on to greater heights.

Step 2: Focus on the positive Once you've created a climate of confidence, you can modify their technique by focusing on the positive. For instance, 'I love the way you do that, especially when you go slowly/quickly/hang off the bedside table while you're doing it.' Use discretion and be specific if possible. And you really need to use your hands to gently direct the action the way you want it.

Defining idea

'*The secret to telling someone they're the worst lover you've ever had, is...not to. Focus on what you want, not what you don't...Start by focusing on yourself, not your partner's [faults]. Make a list of ten things you want more of in bed, ten things you want less of, and ten new things you'd like to try. You have to know what you want in bed in order to get it.*'
TRACEY COX, Supersex

Step 3: Suggest how they could change. Now you can suggest doing it differently. This has to be done with grace and it has to be done lightly, not as if your entire sexual happiness depends on it (remember they can't fail). Say that you've read about something you'd like to try in a book and ask if they would oblige….

42. Try kaizen

Kaizen is a Japanese concept that means, 'Small changes, big differences.' It can revolutionise your love life.

A new persective can perk your relationship up no end. You probably always brush your teeth in the way you perfected in childhood, but if you surprise your brain by brushing your teeth with the other hand, you'll force it to work harder and stay fresher. Changing your routine just slightly – taking a new route to work, kissing friends when you meet rather than hugging them, eating your main meal at noon – will give you a different perspective, a new way of looking at things. The same applies to your love life.

Promise yourself that the next time you make love you will, as far as possible, work on the rule of difference – if you always start with kissing, try flipping your lover over and massaging their shoulders instead; if you prefer to be on top, then lie on your back. You'll feel resistance, as your instincts will be to follow the same old pattern, but

Here's an idea for you...

Ban yourself from coming in your 'normal' way for a month. You'll have to work harder for results, but you'll be forced to be more inventive.

fight it: absolutely nothing is more ruinous to your love life than doing things more or less the same way more or less all the time. Both of you need to try to make sex just a little bit different from the last time or the half a dozen times before that. For example, when you're making love groan 'no' if you always groan 'yes'. Or grab a soft scarf and run it between your partner's legs before rubbing them through the material. Anything at all to reassure your partner that you're not operating on automatic pilot.

Men often wish that their partner would initiate sex more, but what they really mean is initiate sex when they vaguely fancy it. Not, of course, when they're immersed in the cricket, which would be annoying. And annoyed is what your wife feels when you leap on her while she's sorting laundry. Men are generally terrific at bouncing back from rejection because most tend to get lots of practice in adolescence, and they're also willing to put up with their partner taking a moment to get on their sexual wavelength. Women – much more thin-skinned – take that original hesitation on your part as outright rejection and turn away. Perhaps for good. Be

responsive when she's tactile, even
if there's no chance of it
progressing to sex. Her reaching for
your hand while you're shopping
could be the beginning of foreplay
that isn't consummated until after
dinner. Ask her to surprise you just
once in the upcoming month but don't pressurise.

As a rule of thumb:
1. Do something you haven't done in the last month or so every
   single time you make love.
2. Don't come in a certain position if you can remember exactly
   when you last came that way.

43. What's your LQ?

**Imagine you're in the Mastermind chair
and your specialist subject is your lover.
What would be your love quotient (LQ)
score?**

Often we know more about what lights the candle of the person sitting
next to us at work than the person we've chosen to share our lives with.

Years ago I read something in one of John Gray's books that has saved me a lot of grief since. John Gray wrote *Men are from Mars, Women are from Venus*, and the point he made – directed at men – was simple: if your partner adores chocolates and sees them as the eternal proof that you love her, why on earth would you buy her roses? Yet the world is full of guys turning up with bunches of roses and wondering why they get thrown at their head. The moral is simple: if your lover needs chocolates to make them feel loved, give 'em chocolates. It's irrelevant whether you think a bunch of red roses is more romantic. You need to give your partner what they need or you might as well not bother.

Broadly speaking, to successfully love the person we're with we need to understand what they need to feel loved. To keep their love we must give them what they need as far as possible. If you're reading this and wondering what this has to do with sex, my answer to you is, 'Duh! Just about everything.' Loads of couples are having indifferent or absolutely no sex, not because they don't spark off each other but because they haven't felt loved by their partner for years. When your lover's feeling insecure, stressed or worried, how do you make them feel safe and reassured? Does it work? If not, do you

Here's an idea for you...

Feel your partner fails to listen to you? Make sure you've tried sitting down and talking to them calmly. Huffing about or giving them the silent treatment are passive-aggressive ways of getting nowhere. You have to spell it out.

Defining idea

'Sex is a conversation carried out by
another means.'
PETER USTINOV

know what would? If yes, why do
you withhold it from them? Do you
like to play mean just for the hell of
it? It might seem to work and it
might keep you the 'superior'
partner, but the price is high. Your
partner won't be able to trust you and that sort of trust is near
enough essential to keep sex hot between you when the first thrill
has gone.

Would your lover rather have a romantic meal or a wild night out on
the town as a prelude to sex? Do you occasionally indulge them,
even if you'd rather do something else? Emotionally we have to be
given chocolates at least some of the time or we start to shut off
from our partner and get tempted by someone who appears to offer
Milk Tray on demand. If you're with someone for whom chocolate
equals love, all the roses in the world won't fix your relationship or
help you get good sex.

44. Time for bed

I know a woman who tried to convince her lover that the really happening people were giving up sex in favour of sleep.

Competitive tiredness between couples is a relatively new phenomenon and one result of both partners being strung out with exhaustion is no nookie. It's not of course the end of a relationship if you go some time with a lacklustre or indeed non-existent love life. But keep using tiredness as an excuse and before you know it, total inertia has set in.

Having sex when you're tired can start off indifferently and get a whole lot better. And even if it doesn't indifferent sex is better than no sex. Make definite dates when you're going to do it. Make sex that day your priority. See it as a red-letter event.

Reorganising your workloads can help. This quiz gives couples a quick visual reference of who does more around the home. Tick the sex of the partner who most often

Here's an idea for you...

If sex usually takes place just before bed and is generally rushed and unsatisfying because you're both knackered, make a weekly tryst for sex where you go to bed early and enjoy each other. Therapists agree that this 'appointment system' is one of the easiest ways to ease you back into a good sex life.

Defining idea

'He said, "I can't remember when we last had sex." And I said, "Well, I can and that's why we ain't doing it."'
ROSEANNE BARR

undertakes a particular task. This test can be an eye-opener for couples that think they have a pretty equal relationship. If it's not so equal, you have to take steps to delegate or equalise your workload, or your sex life is unlikely to get back to normal any time soon.

	M	F
Getting the children ready for the day	☐	☐
Making breakfast	☐	☐
Making packed lunches	☐	☐
School run	☐	☐
Supervising homework	☐	☐
Teacher's meetings	☐	☐
Immunisations, trips to GP	☐	☐
Dealing with childcare	☐	☐
Bathing children and getting them ready for bed	☐	☐
Bedtime stories	☐	☐
Arranging play dates with other parents	☐	☐
Supermarket shopping	☐	☐
Cooking evening dinner	☐	☐
Clearing house at end of evening	☐	☐
Paying bills	☐	☐
DIY, organising repairs	☐	☐
Cleaning	☐	☐

Taking out rubbish	M ☐	F ☐
Buying children's clothes	M ☐	F ☐
Washing and drying clothes	M ☐	F ☐
Dishwasher loading	M ☐	F ☐
Gardening	M ☐	F ☐
Maintaining and cleaning car	M ☐	F ☐
Organising social life	M ☐	F ☐

You might be reading this and thinking, 'I'm the major breadwinner, I work my butt off and can't do childcare, too.' But you'll have to find some compromise for the sake of your relationship.

45. Body conscious

Learn to express sensuality with your whole body.

Think of ways you can actively be more aware of your bodies and new sensations together.

Step 1
Showering together is one of those things we do at the beginning of a relationship that tails off as the mortgage gets bigger and your hair gets greyer. Give your lover a surprise this week. Wait until it's good and steamy in there. Strip off, step in and start soaping them down.

Here's an idea for you...

Men: instead of using your hands to massage her body, use the sensitive inside of your forearms – it will be a totally different sensation for both of you.

Note for women: put on some gorgeous wispy underwear and step into the shower with him when he's not expecting it. Naked's good. Naked's great. But the feel (and the look!) of the wet fabric plastered against your slick body and the rush he'll get from pushing it aside to get at you should make for a different kind of experience.

Step 2

Look for different ways to surprise each other with unexpected sensations:

- Wear something different from the norm. If you sleep naked, try silk pyjama bottoms. If you always wear a nightdress, change to a simple white cotton brief and vest set.
- Heat up a towel with a hairdryer while your lover's bathing and offer it to them as they come out.
- Take an ice cube and rub it over your lover's bare back or nipples while you're making love, until it melts.

Step 3

Marilyn Monroe's sexual signature note had nothing to do with her looks and everything to do with the electrifying power that touch can have on your average adult male, deprived as he is of all-over, deeply sensual, touch.

Marilyn, so the story goes, would ask her lover to lie on his front and remain very, very still. Once he was in position she'd straddle him from behind and whisper in his ear that he was going to help her to come. Then she'd liberally apply oil on his

Defining idea

'I'm suggesting we call sex something else, and it should include everything from kissing to sitting close together.'
SHERE HITE, sex researcher

back and her body and start slithering up and down on him. Clever Marilyn – what's more likely to make your lover mad for you than letting them know they're driving you mad with lust, while ensuring they get to have a nice little lie down at the same time? Women: try your own version of the Marilyn manoeuvre. Men: to reawaken your sense of touch (the point of this exercise), you could massage your lover while asking her to stay perfectly still. Once she's melting use your imagination.

46. Something for the weekend

Time spent away together intensifies your experiences and your love life.

If your relationship has been in a bit of a slump, a few days away from it all really *is* a perfect chance to recharge your batteries.

Here's an idea for you...

If it's difficult for you to get time away an alternative is to set aside two days together at home, and work out your timetable of love. Everyone can find two days for the sake of their relationship.

Prioritising your love life rather than, say, sightseeing or gastro-pubbing, will fire up your love life for possibly months afterwards. The reason is that a new place lets you reinvent yourselves. You'll be more daring and more focused on each other. And if you have any problem areas, you can plan to sort them out over the weekend.

Here are some ideas for solving two common relationship problems during a typical two-day break. Use them as a model to write out your own 'prescription for love'.

Predicament: You're turning into 'just good friends'.
Goal: Re-establish yourselves as lovers.

Day 1.   Build excitement. Pretend that you are new lovers who aren't ready to move on to the sexual stage of a relationship. Be a little shy, take time with your appearance and see each other as you did in your first days together. See your lover through the same rose-coloured specs that you did in the beginning. Be determined to find them deeply endearing, no matter how much they were irritating you yesterday.

Day 2. Resolve to do something you'll never forget. After the build-up of yesterday, create new shared memories of sex that will stay with both of you when you get home and fuel desire when the rut beckons again. Move mirrors in your hotel room so that you can see yourselves while you have sex. Throw your lover against a wall in a tiny cobbled street. Slip away from the lights and make love on the beach.

Defining idea

'When you do something kinky, it's like, yes, the mango sex. We'll always remember the mango sex...It wasn't even that good, but we remember it. And that's the key – the remembering.'
BETH LAPIDES, American comedian

Predicament: Your love life is predictable.
Goal: To regain the sparkle.

Day 1. Create intimacy. Turn your hotel bedroom into a sensual sanctuary. Spend a couple of hours bathing, showering and massaging each other before dinner. Don't rush into sex (or if you do, maintain the sensual touching afterwards). Live in the moment. Rediscover each other. Hold hands. Maintain eye contact as much as possible. Spend time talking about your feelings about work, family, friends and your relationship. Your aim is to make your lover feel cherished and 'listened to'.

Day 2. Break the patterns. Each write three things you'd like to try on a piece of paper. Take turns to fulfil each other's wishes.

47. In out, in out

Breathing. You do it every single minute of your life. Boy, have you been taking it for granted.

Tturn the simple breathing action into a way to heighten sexual pleasure and get closer to your partner.

The 'complete' breath. Yogic breathing is to draw breath in, hold the breath in your lungs, exhale and then pause before breathing again. Practise this and then breathe in for one count, hold for four counts, breathe out for two counts and pause. Repeat this until it comes naturally.

Focusing on lurve. In the Tantric tradition, the inward breath is associated with energy and the outward breath with consciousness. This is a good basis for a mini-meditation session before you make love. Concentrate on taking in energy with each inward breath and, with each outward breath, bringing your concentration to bear on how you're feeling right here, right now.

Here's an idea for you...

If you're wound up, try using breathing techniques to de-stress yourself. They're the basis of all meditation, as well as improving communication with your loved one.

Breathing in Unison. This simple breathing exercise is a quick way to improve communication. Try it once a day (oh, alright then, as often as you remember), in bed or out, clothed or not. Hold on to each other and regulate your breaths. Let thoughts drift away as they float into your mind. Just be with each other. Lie in bed, 'spooned' around one another, and simply breathe in unison. During the two weeks that I 'researched' this with my husband, we spent hours writing lists, talking deeply, having sex at odd times and in odd positions, massaging each other and even venturing to a salsa class.

For those who like this, try heart breathing. Sit on your bed in a comfortable position facing each other. Place your hands flat on your chest between your breasts (above the heart chakra). Close your eyes. Now breathe as detailed under 'The complete breath' above. Imagine you're drawing love in with each breath and, while holding it in your lungs, feel it nourishing your body and spirit. Finally, when you breathe out imagine your breath leaving your body as a wave of love rolling over and around your partner. Open your eyes and look at your partner while you breathe together.

Defining idea.

'Your breath is a bridge between your body, feelings and thoughts, your energy, your past and your present. How we breathe directly affects every cell of our body, and it also influences how we feel emotionally. As such, the breath is also a vehicle for expansion and ecstasy.'
LEONORA LIGHTWOMAN, Tantric teacher and author

113

48. Just say 'no'

There's saying 'no' and there's saying 'no' nicely. Two very different things.

Every relationship has its sexual deserts when sex is off the cards. This can hurt your relationship. If your partner approaches you and you feel ambivalent about having sex, the best advice is to go along with it for a while and try to get yourself in the mood (with their help, of course). If, however, you fail to rise onto that wave of lust, all you can do is gaze into their eyes tenderly and say, 'Sorry, it isn't working for me tonight, but I promise that tomorrow we'll do the deed.' Sex therapists pretty much agree that rejection is easier to take if there's a definite date set for retrial.

But what if you know that tomorrow you're not going to want to have sex either? You're in a sexual desert. Do you want to find your oasis?

Here's an idea for you...

If you and your partner haven't had sex for a month, sit down, look into his/her eyes and ask why. The longer you go without sex, the easier it becomes to do without it. The more you do it, the more you'll want to.

'Yes' to the oasis. Is there a medical reason that one or both of you has gone off sex? Is it because one or both of you is having a mid-life crisis? Deal with that first.

'No' to the oasis. Tricky one this. You've gone off sex. You don't fancy your partner anymore. You can't be bothered to try. When they approach you, you simply don't want to do it.

Defining idea

'Marriage, if it is to survive, must be treated as the beginning, not as the happy ending.'
FEDERICO FELLINI

- Decide on a time when you're going to get physical and then do all you can to get yourself in the mood, such as a bath, delicious food, candles or a chat. Enjoy each other. Don't expect mind-bending lust – mildly being up for it is good enough.
- Being physically close without having penetrative sex can eventually kick start your libido. In fact, when you've been together for a while, you often need physical proximity to start feeling desire.

The bottom line is, if you can't be bothered to do all you can to get yourself and your partner in the mood for sex then you're a rotten lover. What's loving about a person who doesn't at least try? This is brutal, but it's true. Your lover is almost certain to get depressed and unconfident – both traits are hell to live with and unlikely to endear them to you. Keeping your sex life extant is as important for your mental health as theirs.

49. Developing sexual mystique

Yes, it's possible. Even if you've shared a bathroom for years.

Just remember: 'vive la différence'.'Male and female are different,' says relationship counsellor Paula Hall. 'And we've known since the sixties that if a couple want a stable relationship, it's worth working at maintaining that difference. It's what keeps the electric buzz between them.' She points out that studies by psychologists have already picked up on the dangers of becoming too alike. 'We call it "enmeshment" when couples become too similar,' says Hall. 'It's been known for a long time that it can have a detrimental impact on desire.'

Here's an idea for you...

In a nutshell, make it a habit that one night a week you do your own thing, no matter how busy you are. Remember, spending too much time inside together is terrible for your love life.

You can be all things to a partner, but not to a lover. They cannot be all things to you.

There's an art to this. One friend is just a little bit cool with her husband every three or four months or so. 'Nothing serious,' she said, 'I'd just switch off from him a bit. Seem a little bit less easily pleased. A bit more interested in talking to my friends on the phone. Lock myself in the bathroom. Submerge myself in a book. Really trivial stuff. Works like a charm. Within a week, he'll be suggesting weekends away in Paris and voluntarily arranging babysitting so we can go out to dinner.'

Defining idea

'An absence, the declining of an invitation to dinner, an unintentional, unconscious harshness are of more service than all the cosmetics and fine clothes in the world.'
MARCEL PROUST

All this withdrawing interest sounds suspiciously like game-playing – and you know what, it is! You can fake it a little bit like my interviewee, but it doesn't always work. What does always work is if both partners do it for real – keep interested in life, stay full of vim and brio for other projects, remain engaged with people outside of their relationship and be passionate about the world. Then, and here is the important bit, they bring that energy home and translate it into passion for each other. They do that by talking about their lives with such enthusiasm that their partners can't help getting a kick out of their enthusiasm, charm, intelligence and all-round top-quality personality.

The least you need to do...
Rule 1. All couples fall into a pattern of 'we don't do that'. But if you fancy doing something different, suggest it anyway. Don't argue if

they say 'no'. The point has been made. You've reinforced in both your minds that you're different individuals.

Rule 2. Support your partner as much as possible when they're trying to be an individual.

Rule 3. Be yourself. Don't take on his interests and hobbies unless they genuinely interest you, too. We're equal but we're not the same.

50. Burnout

That's what we call it when your relationship is a mess and you just don't care. How do you know when you're dealing with burnout?

Problem: Too many people want a bit of you.

Solution: Set boundaries and cut down on commitments.

People who don't set boundaries often end up playing out their frustrations in the bedroom: 'You don't give me what I need, so you won't get what you need.' This is equally true for the woman who withdraws sex as the man who, although he wants sex, isn't affectionate because he feels overburdened with responsibility. When you're too tired for sex or to give your partner what they need to feel good, the answer is to spend time cutting loose from all commitment. Time alone gives you a sense of balance and renewal, which can give you more energy.

How do you find that time? By setting boundaries. Here's what Dr Alan Altman says in his book *Making Love the Way We Used To, or Better*: 'You can help others, but you do not have to be everyone's answer to everything. Sometimes saying no is a gift to the other person, who grows and becomes stronger by learning more self-reliance.'

Here's an idea for you...

Read books that thrilled you in your teens. Read books that make you horny. Listen to music that makes you feel sexual (or free, romantic, wild, independent). Play it loud and play it often. Dance around your bedroom.

Problem: You're bored with life.
Solution: Rediscover your passion and revel in pleasure.
You may well be having a mid-life crisis – even if you're only 27. Tell your partner honestly, 'I'm worried. I'm rather fed up with everything. I don't have juice for anything much, and with your help I want to get back my va-va-voom.' Then you can negotiate more time for yourself, more holidays together. Whatever it takes to get more pleasure into your life, because pleasure is the only cure for a mid-life crisis and all other forms of burnout. Your partner might not like some of your ideas – they're never going to think that a Harley Davidson is a great idea and they're certainly not going

Defining ideas

'Sex without love is an empty experience, but, as empty experiences go, it's one of the best.'
WOODY ALLEN

to warm to the leather chaps. But if yours is a good healthy relationship then they'll live with whatever it takes to return you to the happy love bunny you were of yore. Unless, of course, it threatens them or the relationship, in which case you don't have a healthy relationship and you need the sort of help that's outside the scope of this slender tome. Good luck with the therapy.

51. Pressure – it's not a dirty word

Or rather, if you're doing it right, it can be.

For times when you want to feast on a banquet of love, there is massage. First, select your oil. You can buy massage oils premixed or create your own blend by adding eight to ten drops of oil (or a mixture of oils) to three dessertspoons of a base oil such as almond. Good oils for sensual massage are geranium, which is uplifting and grounding; lavender, which is relaxing and soothing; sandalwood, which is warming and encouraging; and ylang ylang, which is sensual and erotic. Burning the same combination of oils as you massage will heighten the experience for your lover.

Choose a warm, comfortable place in your home. Put on some gentle music and lower the lights. Take some oil and warm it between your palms. Then start working it into your partner's back. Use firm gliding strokes over the large muscles of the shoulder blades, then work down the sides to the base of the spine and then work upwards using the balls of your thumbs to apply pressure on either side of the spine. The secret of applying pressure is to channel the strength of your body through the balls of your thumbs. Lean into your lover's body but apply pressure only to the meaty parts of the body (but not the belly). Don't apply pressure on hard bony areas.

Continue with sweeping movements alternated by gentle pressure across the back, buttocks and the back of legs. Use long strokes along the arms and gently pull at each finger in turn. Try different pressures. Use fists to apply heavier kneading movements to the buttocks. Apply very light blows across the back. Then alternate with gentle fingertip stroking.

Here's an idea for you

Maintain skin-to-skin contact throughout the massage. Cup one hand on your lover's back while you pour more oil so that the back of your hand maintains this contact.

Defining ideas

'To lovers, touch is metamorphosis. All the parts of their bodies seem to change, and seem to become something different and better.'
JOHN CHEEVER, American writer

Concentrate on your lover's body and giving it pleasure. Ask for a little feedback. For example, does your partner want a gentler or firmer stroke? But don't talk too much. Allow your partner to relax into the massage.

Ask your partner to turn over. Holding their head steady with your knees and massaging their face is particularly relaxing. Don't apply heavy pressure to the stomach. Brush but don't directly touch their genitals – the oils may irritate sensitive areas.

Short cut to Bliss

If you don't have the time to indulge in a full body treat, give a foot massage instead.

Bathe your lover's feet. A few drops of peppermint oil in a basin refresh instantly and keep things fresh for you. Then ask them to sit while you kneel at their feet, with a towel over your knees to cradle each foot in turn. Massage oil over one foot. Apply pressure through your thumbs systematically all over the soles of the feet. Concentrate particularly on the fleshy parts of each toe in turn and gently pull and rotate each one.

52. The least you need to do...

...to keep your relationship minty fresh.

This idea contains the three golden rules of a healthy relationship. Couples that spend time together, and anticipate and plan for those times, find it hard to lose interest in one another.

Rule 1: Daily...
How is your partner feeling right now? What's happening at work? How are their relationships with friends, colleagues, siblings, parents? Carve out fifteen minutes of every day to talk. Go to bed before your usual time or get up earlier and have a coffee together so you can touch base.

Kiss each other every morning before you get out of bed. Take the time for a swift cuddle. Breathe deeply. Hold tight. Do the same at night. Never take your physical intimacy for granted. In this Vale of Tears we call life, you found each other. Pretty amazing. Worth acknowledging that with at least a daily hug, methinks.

Here's an idea for you...

Look for easy ways to cheer your partner up. Pick up a tub of her favourite ice-cream on the way home from work. Run him a bath and bring him a beer. Sappy gestures work – they build up a huge bank of goodwill that couples can draw on when life gets stressful.

Rule 2: Weekly...

Go out with each other once a week where humanly possible. Once a fortnight is the bare minimum. According to the experts, this is the most important thing you can do. Couples who keep dating, keep mating.

Spending too long sloping around the same house does something to a couple's sexual interest in each other and what it does generally isn't good. So get out, preferably after making some small effort to tart yourself up so you're visually pleasing to your partner. Let them see why they bothered with you in the first place.

Rule 3: Monthly...

Go for a mini-adventure – shared memories cement your relationship. Make your adventure as mad or staid as you like. It really doesn't matter what it is, as long as it's not your usual 'date'. What's the point? You see your partner coping with new environments and new skills and that keeps you interested in them. And them in you. Simple.

Research shows quite clearly that one of the defining differences between strong couples and 'drifting' couples is the amount of effort and time they spend on their shared pursuits. All of us have heard the advice, 'Spend more time with each other being as interesting as possible.' But how many couples do you know who actually do it? I'm prepared to bet that those who do seem happiest.

Defining idea

'Good sex begins when your clothes are still on.'
MASTERS and JOHNSON, sex research pioneers

brilliant ideas

Perfect romance: 52 brilliant little ideas for finding and keeping a lover is published by Infinite Ideas, creators of the acclaimed 52 Brilliant Ideas series. If you found this book helpful, you may want to take advantage of this special offer exclusive to all readers of *Perfect romance*. Choose any two books from the selection below and you'll get one of them free of charge*. See overleaf for prices and details on how to place your order.

- **Be incredibly sexy:** 52 brilliant ideas for sizzling sensuality
- **Inspired creative writing:** 52 brilliant ideas from the master wordsmiths
- **Look gorgeous always:** 52 brilliant ideas to find it, fake it and flaunt it
- **Upgrade your brain:** 52 brilliant ideas for everyday genius
- **Re-energise your sex life:** 52 brilliant ideas to put the zing back into your lovemaking
- **Stress proof your life:** 52 brilliant ideas for taking control
- **Lose weight and stay slim:** Secrets of fad-free dieting
- **Secrets of wine:** Insider insights into the real world of wine

For more detailed information on these books and others published by Infinite Ideas please visit www.infideas.com

*Postage at £2.75 per delivery address is additional.

Choose any two titles from below and receive one of them free.

Qty	Title	RRP
	Be incredibly sexy	£12.99
	Inspired creative writing	£12.99
	Look gorgeous always	£12.99
	Upgrade your brain	£12.99
	Re-energise your sex life	£12.99
	Stress proof your life	£12.99
	Lose weight and stay slim	£12.99
	Secrets of wine	£12.99

Subtract £12.99 if ordering two titles

Add £2.75 postage per delivery address

Final TOTAL

Name: ....

Delivery address: ....

....

....

E-mail:...........................Tel (in case of problems): ....

By post Fill in all relevant details, cut out or copy this page and send along with a cheque made payable to Infinite Ideas. Send to: *Perfect romance* BOGOF, Infinite Ideas, 36 St Giles, Oxford OX1 3LD. **Credit card orders over the telephone** Call +44 (0) 1865 514 888. Lines are open 9am to 5pm Monday to Friday. Just mention the promotion code 'PRAD06.'

Please note that no payment will be processed until your order has been dispatched. Goods are dispatched through Royal Mail within 14 working days, when in stock. We never forward personal details on to third parties or bombard you with junk mail. This offer is valid for UK and RoI residents only. Any questions or comments please contact us on 01865 514 888 or email info@infideas.com.